COST SAVVY
SECURE
CLOUD

A BUSINESS OWNERS GUIDE TO CLOUD SECURITY, SAVINGS AND AI EVOLUTION

PREITY GUPTA

Copyright © 2024 Preity Gupta

ISBN: 978-81-19682-32-4

Published by: Beeja House

Printed By: Repro India Pvt. Ltd.

First Printing Edition 2024

Dedication

To my beloved Parents and Brother,

Your unwavering support, endless encouragement, and timeless guidance have been the cornerstone of my journey. As I embark on the voyage of writing my book, I carry with me the values and lessons you have instilled in me. With deepest gratitude and admiration, I dedicate this work to you, whose boundless love has shaped my lives and empowered me to reach for the stars.

To my Mentors,

Your wisdom, encouragement, and unwavering support have fuelled my journey, empowering me to delve deep into the complexities of business networks, security frameworks, and innovative technologies. With heartfelt gratitude, I honour your invaluable contributions, which have shaped not only this book but also my understanding of the dynamic landscape of cloud computing and cloud security with cost management.

Purpose of Book

If you believe that *"Security measures are inherently expensive"*, *"We're too small to be a target"*, *"Cloud providers handle all security"*, or *"Firewalls and antivirus are enough"* then you've chosen the perfect book to delve into.

In an era where cloud transformation is not just an ambition but a fundamental necessity for businesses, the goal of financial resilience and expansion faces a critical need for robust cloud security with Generative AI while managing costs effectively. This need is where my journey as an author begins and this book, "Cost Savvy Secure Cloud" finds its purpose.

As a seasoned expert in the fields of technology and business strategy, I wrote this book to address a crucial gap I observed in the market: the lack of comprehensive resources that interconnect the complexities of cloud security, cost management, and the emerging field of Generative AI (GenAI). This guide is a response to the numerous conversations I've had with business owners and CXOs who expressed their struggles with balancing the high need for cybersecurity with the pressure of financial efficiency in a rapidly evolving digital landscape.

In a world where businesses are increasingly dependent on digital platforms, especially cloud computing, the spectrum of cyber threats expands, ranging from data breaches and malware attacks to sophisticated phishing and insider threats. These risks carry severe real-world consequences, including financial loss, reputational damage, and legal complications.

My motivation for writing this book stemmed from a desire to empower business leaders with the knowledge and tools necessary to navigate these challenges effectively.

This book is unique in its approach. It goes beyond the traditional scope of business literature by offering a holistic view that combines strategic insights with practical, actionable solutions. It addresses the crucial need for businesses to understand and optimize cloud security with Generative AI and cost management in an era dominated by technological advancements and sophisticated cyber threats.

In these pages, we explore the strategic benefits of migrating to the cloud, and the need for cloud security that includes enhanced data encryption, sophisticated access controls, and network security along with the confidentiality, integrity and availability, needed for business and its innovation. We delve into the Zero Trust model, emphasizing its criticality in a cloud environment where traditional security perimeters have dissolved. The book also provides a deep dive into how Generative AI is transforming the business landscape, offering new opportunities for efficiency and growth.

What sets this guide apart is its timeliness and relevance. As technological advancements continue constantly and cyber threats evolve aggressively, mastering cloud security and cost management is not a choice but a necessity for sustainable business success. This book is a tribute to that reality, born out of my passion for empowering leaders in the digital age.

As you turn these pages, you will embark on a journey that is not just educational but transformational. This book is designed to be a strategic partner, offering insights and tools that will enable you to turn the challenges of cloud security and cost into opportunities for innovation and growth.

Welcome to your comprehensive guide, a book born out of necessity and shaped by the needs of modern business leaders, ready to navigate the complexities of cloud security, cost management and Generative AI.

Introduction

Welcome to the journey of exploring Cloud Security, Cost Management, and Generative AI Integration in the realm of modern business. In this book, we delve into the intricate dynamics that shape the security landscape of cloud-based environments and the strategic considerations that underpin successful implementations.

Chapter 1: Business Owners and Their Dilemma Regarding Cloud Security

In the opening chapter, we confront the challenges faced by business owners in navigating the complexities of cloud security. Through case studies and analyses, we uncover the misconceptions surrounding security responsibilities and highlight the critical role of cloud security in business growth.

Chapter 2: Striking the right balance among Cloud Network Security, Cost Management, and Generative AI Security

Chapter 2 explores the delicate balance between cloud network security, cost management, and the integration of generative AI security solutions. Through financial analysis and real-world examples, we discern the optimal strategies for maximizing security efficacy while minimizing operational costs.

Chapter 3: Cost efficient Cloud Network Security Components

Here, we delve into the essential components of cost-efficient cloud network security. From robust antivirus software to streamlined monitoring processes, we identify key strategies for optimizing security investments without compromising effectiveness.

Chapter 4: Business Transformation through the Implementation of Generative AI

Chapter 4 unveils the transformative potential of generative AI in bolstering business resilience and continuity. Through case studies and examinations of AI-driven security tools, we illustrate how businesses can leverage artificial intelligence to stay ahead of emerging threats.

Chapter 5: Governance for Business Advancement

In this chapter, we explore governance frameworks for fostering secure, efficient, ethical, and innovative business operations in the cloud. From security governance to compliance management, we delineate the essential principles and practices for effective governance in the digital age.

Chapter 6: Exploring Business Success Stories Achieved through the Implementation of Cloud Network Security, Efficient Cost Management, and the Integration of Generative AI

Chapter 6 presents real-world success stories of businesses that have harnessed the power of cloud network security, cost management, and generative AI integration to achieve remarkable outcomes. Through these narratives, we glean valuable insights into the transformative potential of strategic security investments.

Chapter 7 – Conclusion

In the concluding chapter, we reflect on the key learnings and insights garnered throughout our exploration of cloud security, cost management, and generative AI integration. We outline actionable steps for businesses to embark on their journey towards enhanced security, efficiency, and innovation in the cloud era.

Exercise your knowledge, explore the case studies, and embark on a transformative journey with us!

Contents

Chapter 1

Business Owners and Their Dilemma Regarding Cloud Security

In a world where digital breaches are not a question of 'if' but 'when,' understanding cloud security and cost management is not just important – it's indispensable. Business owners' dilemmas require a thoughtful and strategic approach. Business owners should assess their unique business requirements, risk tolerance, and long-term goals to make informed decisions about cloud security. Regularly reassessing the security landscape and staying updated on best practices will contribute to a more resilient and secure cloud environment.

Challenges Business Owners Face in Tackling the Cloud Security

There is a misconception that "Security is a Technology Issue, not a Business Issue": Security should be viewed as a business issue that affects the organization's overall health, reputation, and success. Business owners face a challenge when it comes to cloud security, balancing the benefits of cloud computing with the potential risks and challenges associated with securing digital assets. Here are some common challenges that business owners may encounter in the realm of cloud security:

- **Cost v/s Security:** Business owners struggle to balance the need for robust security measures with the desire to minimize costs.
  Misconception: "Security measures are inherently expensive".

- **Shared Responsibility Misunderstanding**: Some business owners may incorrectly assume that the cloud service provider is solely responsible for security.
  Misconception: Cloud providers handle all security.

- **Limited Resources vs. Comprehensive Security:** Small and medium-sized businesses have limited resources for cybersecurity, making it challenging to implement comprehensive security measures.
  Misconception: "We're too small to be a target"

- **Understanding Complex Cloud Environments:** Many business owners, especially those not deeply versed in IT, find it challenging to fully understand the complexities of cloud environments, including different service models (IaaS, PaaS, SaaS) and deployment types (public, private, hybrid).
  Misconception: "Cloud is just someone else's computer"

- **Selecting the Right Cloud Provider:** With numerous cloud service providers offering a range of services, choosing the right provider that aligns with the specific needs, budget, and compliance requirements of the business can be daunting.
  Misconception: "All cloud providers are the same" or "Choosing the largest cloud provider is always the best option"

- **Data Security and Privacy Concerns:** Protecting sensitive data from breaches, unauthorized access, and cyber-attacks is a primary concern. Business owners often worry about the security of data in transit and at rest, as well as the provider's data encryption policies.
  Misconception: "Firewalls and antivirus are enough"

- **Integration with Existing Systems:** Integrating cloud services with existing on-premises infrastructure or other cloud-based tools can be complex. Ensuring compatibility and smooth interoperability without disrupting current operations is a key challenge.
  Misconception: "Integration with the cloud will automatically improve system performance"

- **Convenience vs. Control:** Cloud services offer convenience and scalability, but some business owners may worry about relinquishing control over their data and infrastructure.
  Misconception: "Convenience and control are mutually exclusive"

- **Innovation vs. Security:** Business owners, especially in tech-driven industries, prioritize rapid innovation but worry about the security implications of adopting new technologies.
  Misconception: "Innovation and security are inherently at odds with each other"

- **Compliance vs. Agility:** Meeting industry compliance requirements is crucial, but business owners fear that compliance efforts could slow down the agility and flexibility offered by cloud services.

Misconception: *"Compliance and agility are incompatible"*

- **Scalability and Flexibility Issues:** While cloud services are inherently scalable, predicting future needs and selecting a service that can scale effectively with the growth of the business is challenging.
  Misconception: *"While scalability and flexibility are related, they are not the same"*

- **Lack of Expertise and Resources:** Small to medium-sized businesses may lack the in-house expertise required to manage and secure cloud environments effectively, leading to the need for external consultants or more comprehensive service packages.
  Misconception: *"Cloud security measures are only relevant for large enterprises with extensive resources and dedicated security teams"*

- **User Experience vs. Security Measures:** Business owners have a dilemma that implementing stringent security measures impacts the user experience, potentially leading to frustration among employees or customers.
  Misconception: *"User experience and security measures are inherently at odds with each other"*

- **Lack of Awareness:** Some business owners may not fully understand the risks and importance of cloud security.
  Misconception: *"Lack of awareness about cloud security is primarily a technical issue"*

- **Managing Multi-cloud and Hybrid Environments:** Businesses using a combination of different cloud services or a mix of cloud and on-premises solutions face additional complexity in managing and securing these environments.
  Misconception: "Multi-cloud and hybrid environments is that they are inherently more complex"

- **Ensuring Continuous Availability and Disaster Recovery:** Business owners need to ensure that their cloud service provides robust disaster recovery and maintains high availability to prevent downtime, which can be costly and damaging to operations.
  Misconception: "Continuous availability and disaster recovery is that it's solely an IT responsibility"

- **Dealing with Vendor Lock-in:** There is often a concern about becoming too reliant on a single cloud provider, which can lead to challenges if the business decides to switch providers or needs to integrate with services from another provider.
  Misconception: "Vendor lock-in is that it's an unavoidable consequence of adopting cloud services"

By recognizing these challenges and implementing proactive strategies, business owners can enhance their ability to tackle the cloud security puzzle effectively. Regular reassessment of security measures and staying informed about evolving threats are essential components of a robust cloud security strategy.

Case Study: On Misconception that "Security is a Technology Issue, not a Business Issue"

I once worked closely with a mid-sized technology company that specialized in software development and digital solutions for various industries. As digital technologies and cloud services became increasingly critical to their operations, the company recognized the importance of cybersecurity in safeguarding sensitive data, intellectual property, and reputation. However, a prevailing misconception within the organization was that security was solely a technology issue and not a concern for the entire business.

Here's what I observed:

Lack of Executive Leadership Involvement: The company's executive leadership viewed cybersecurity as a technical matter best handled by the IT department. There was minimal participation from senior management in setting strategic security objectives or integrating security into business processes. Consequently, security initiatives lacked executive sponsorship and failed to align with broader business goals.

Limited Budget Allocation for Security: Due to the perception that security was primarily a technology issue, the company allocated a restricted budget to cybersecurity initiatives. The focus was mainly on purchasing and implementing security tools, neglecting investments in security awareness training, risk management, and incident response capabilities. This narrow focus hindered the organization's ability to address security comprehensively and adapt to evolving threats.

Siloed Approach to Security: Different departments operated in isolation, lacking effective communication and collaboration on security matters. Business units prioritized speed-to-market and innovation over security considerations, leading to the deployment of vulnerable software and services. The absence of a unified security strategy and governance framework increased the organization's exposure to cyber risks and threats.

Compliance-Centric Mindset: The company's approach to security was primarily compliance-driven, focusing on meeting regulatory requirements rather than addressing broader business risks and threats. While compliance standards provided essential guidelines, they often represented the minimum baseline for cybersecurity. This mindset resulted in a false sense of security and left critical assets vulnerable to exploitation.

Lack of Security Culture: Despite investments in technology solutions, the company struggled to foster a strong security culture across the organization. Employees perceived security as solely an IT responsibility rather than a shared responsibility across all business functions. The absence of security awareness training, incident response protocols, and clear accountability mechanisms further undermined the organization's ability to mitigate insider threats and human errors.

Strategies Implemented

Executive Leadership Engagement: Engaged Senior management actively in cybersecurity governance and decision-making processes, and demonstrated a commitment to prioritized security as a strategic business imperative.

Integrated Risk Management: Adopted a risk-based approach to cybersecurity that considered the organization's overall risk appetite, business objectives, and regulatory requirements was crucial.

Investment in People and Processes: Allocated resources for security awareness training, talent development, and process improvement initiatives aimed at enhancing organizational resilience and response capabilities were necessary.

Collaborative Governance: Established cross-functional committees and working groups to promote collaboration, communication, and knowledge-sharing across departments was essential.

Continuous Improvement: Implementing a culture of continuous improvement and learning, where security practices were regularly reviewed, evaluated, and updated in response to emerging threats and evolving business needs was vital.

By challenging the misconception that "Security is a Technology Issue, not a Business Issue," the company could strengthen its cybersecurity posture, enhance stakeholder confidence, and safeguard its reputation and assets in an increasingly digital and interconnected world.

Significance of Cloud Security for Types of Business Owners

Imagine, in a blink, years of hard-earned business growth and reputation being compromised by a single cybersecurity breach. This is not just a hypothetical scenario but a stark reality for businesses today. It's important to recognize that virtually every modern business can benefit from cloud computing and, by extension, needs robust cloud security. Here's a breakdown of various types of business owners who should be particularly mindful of cloud security:

- **E-commerce Business Owners:** These businesses handle sensitive customer information, including credit card numbers and personal details, making them prime targets for cyberattacks. Secure cloud services ensure the safety of customer data and maintain trust.

- **Tech Startups:** Startups, especially in the tech sector, often rely on cloud computing for scalability and flexibility. As these businesses grow rapidly, they need to ensure their data and intellectual property are protected against breaches and theft.

- **Healthcare Providers:** Healthcare professionals who store patient records electronically must comply with strict regulations like HIPAA in the U.S. Cloud security is vital for protecting patient privacy and ensuring compliance with these regulations.

- **Financial Services Firms:** Banks, investment firms, and insurance companies deal with highly sensitive financial data. These businesses require robust cloud security measures to prevent data breaches that could lead to financial loss and reputational damage.

- **Educational Institutions:** Schools and universities increasingly use cloud services for online learning and student data management. They need to protect this data from unauthorized access while ensuring compliance with educational privacy laws.

- **Retail Business Owners:** Retailers, both online and brick-and-mortar, use cloud services for inventory management, sales tracking, and customer relationship management. Secure cloud solutions are essential to protect business data and customer information.

- **Manufacturing Companies:** Manufacturers who employ cloud-based solutions for supply chain management, product design, and operations need to ensure their proprietary information and trade secrets are securely stored and managed.

- **Professional Service Providers:** Lawyers, accountants, and consultants who handle confidential client information can benefit from the cloud for data storage and collaboration. However, they must ensure that client confidentiality is maintained through secure cloud practices.

- **Creative Industries:** Businesses in the creative sector, such as advertising, media, and design, often rely on the cloud for storing large files and collaborative projects. Ensuring the security of these assets is crucial to maintaining intellectual property rights and client trust.

- **Hospitality and Travel Industry:** Companies in the hospitality and travel sector manage large amounts of customer data, from personal details to payment information. Secure cloud solutions are necessary to protect this data and ensure smooth operations.

- **Global Enterprises:** Large multinational corporations with a global presence need to address complex security challenges related to data residency, international regulations, and the diverse threat landscape in different regions.

In summary, cloud security is relevant for a broad spectrum of business owners, and its importance increases when dealing with sensitive data, compliance requirements, and the need to maintain customer trust. Regardless of the industry, every business should assess its unique risk profile and implement appropriate security measures to protect its digital assets in the cloud.

Choosing the Right Cloud Provider for Cost Efficiency and Business Growth

The cloud is not merely a tool, it's a catalyst for transformation, innovation, and growth. In embracing cloud computing, you are not just optimizing costs or enhancing efficiency; you are opening doors to new possibilities, from global expansion to groundbreaking innovations. Some of the key points to be considered while choosing the right cloud provider for cost efficiency and business growth are:

- **Pricing Structure**: Evaluate the pricing models of different cloud providers. Some may offer pay-as-you-go models, while others might have fixed or tiered pricing. Compare these structures to your usage patterns to determine which is most cost-effective for your business.

- **Scalability and Flexibility**: Assess how easily each provider allows the scaling of resources. Providers that offer seamless scalability can be more cost-effective as you only pay for what you use, and they can better support business growth.

- **Performance and Reliability**: Compare the performance metrics such as uptime guarantees and the historical performance of each provider. Reliable performance is critical for business continuity and can indirectly affect costs through downtime or slow operations.

- **Data Storage and Management Costs**: Examine the costs associated with data storage, data transfer, and management. These can vary significantly between providers and can impact overall costs, especially for data-intensive businesses.

- **Security and Compliance**: Review the security measures and compliance standards each provider adheres to. Ensuring data protection and regulatory compliance can prevent costly legal issues and data breaches.

- **Customer Support and Service Level Agreements (SLAs)**: Analyse the level of customer support offered. Strong support and favourable SLAs can prevent or quickly resolve issues, minimizing operational disruptions.

- **Integration Capabilities**: Consider how well each cloud service integrates with your existing systems and tools. Effective integration can reduce costs associated with system modifications or additional software purchases.

- **Customization and Control**: Determine the level of customization and control each provider offers. More control can mean more efficient use of resources, potentially optimizing costs.

- **Innovative Solutions and Advanced Technologies**: Look into each provider's offerings in terms of innovative solutions, such as AI, machine learning, and analytics tools. These technologies can drive business advancement and offer a competitive edge.

- **Market Reputation and Expertise**: Evaluate the provider's reputation and expertise in the market. A provider with a strong reputation for reliability and innovation can be a valuable partner for business growth.

- **Ecosystem and Network**: Consider the provider's ecosystem, including partnerships and network, which can offer additional resources and opportunities for business advancement.

- **Long-term Viability**: Assess the long-term viability of the provider. Choosing a provider with a strong future outlook is crucial for sustained business growth.

It's clear that the journey into cloud computing is not just a leap into a new technological realm, but a strategic step towards redefining the future of your business. The process of choosing the right cloud networking service is akin to navigating a vast ocean of possibilities. Each decision you make aligns your sails towards the winds of progress and success.

Security Breach – Business Owners Negligence

Is it imperative to conduct both security and financial assessments for business development?

Marriott, one of the leading hotel chains, made the strategic decision to merge with Starwood Hotels in 2016. As a business, they aimed to enhance their core competencies and expand their operations. Consequently, they selected Starwood Hotels and conducted a comprehensive financial analysis, including purchase price allocation, cash and stock calculations, goodwill assessment, synergy calculations, and more.

However, they overlooked the importance of security analysis, leading to significant consequences two years after the merger. They discovered that hackers had compromised 500 million customer records, including personal information and credit card details. The root causes like Outdated network configurations, open RDP ports, lack of multifactor authentication, absence of endpoint protection, outdated antivirus software, patch management deficiencies, and other security vulnerabilities allowed hackers to infiltrate their infrastructure.

As a result, Marriott incurred substantial losses in the form of recovery costs, reputation damage, and legal penalties. They spent $30 million on recovery efforts for identity protection and customer satisfaction, faced a $2 billion drop in stock prices due to reputation damage, and received a $120 million fine for breaching British customer privacy laws. Their negligence toward security proved to be detrimental to their business growth.

The solution lies in conducting a comprehensive network infrastructure assessment and implementing necessary security measures aligned with security architecture. Security architecture encompasses on-premises security, cloud security, hybrid security, and multi-cloud security. Therefore, it is crucial to prioritize security assessments alongside financial evaluations for sustained business growth.

Summary:

It is misconception that "Security is a Technology Issue, not a Business Issue"

- *Several prevalent challenges that confront business owners in the domain of cloud security include Lack of Awareness, Misunderstanding of Shared Responsibility, Complex Cloud Environment Understanding, Cloud Provider Selection, Integration with Existing Systems, and Management of Multi-cloud and Hybrid Environments, among others.*

- *Cloud Security holds paramount importance for various types of Business Owners, including those in Healthcare, Startups, Financial sectors, and more.*

- *The process of selecting the appropriate Cloud provider hinges upon specific parameters and considerations.*

- *A single instance of negligence from the Business Owner can result in the loss of hard-earned capital accumulated over years due to a solitary security breach, leading to reputational damage, recovery expenses, and legal ramifications.*

Exercise:

Objective: The objective of this exercise is to assess the current state of cloud security within your business, identify key challenges, and develop actionable strategies to improve cloud security posture.

Steps:

- **Gather Stakeholders**: Bring together key stakeholders from various departments, including IT, security, compliance, and business leadership.

- **Define Objectives**: Clearly define the objectives of the workshop, emphasizing the importance of addressing cloud security challenges to protect sensitive data and mitigate risks.

- **Review Current Infrastructure**: Conduct a comprehensive review of your organization's current cloud infrastructure, including services, platforms, and configurations across all cloud environments (e.g., AWS, Azure, Google Cloud).

- **Identify Assets and Risks**: Identify critical assets, data repositories, and potential security risks associated with cloud usage. Consider data sensitivity, compliance requirements, and the potential impact of security breaches.

- **Brainstorm Challenges**: Facilitate a discussion to identify specific challenges and pain points related to cloud security. Encourage participants to share their experiences, concerns, and observations.

- **Prioritize Challenges**: Prioritize the identified challenges based on their potential impact on business operations, compliance requirements, and data security.

- **Breakout Groups**: Divide participants into small breakout groups to focus on addressing specific challenges. Each group should be tasked with developing strategies and solutions to mitigate the identified challenges.

- **Develop Action Plan**: Reconvene and have each breakout group present their proposed strategies and solutions. Discuss the feasibility, resource requirements, and potential impact of each proposed action.

- **Prioritize Actions**: Prioritize the proposed actions based on their effectiveness, feasibility, and alignment with business objectives. Identify quick wins and long-term initiatives to improve cloud security posture.

- **Assign Responsibilities**: Assign responsibilities for implementing the agreed-upon actions to relevant stakeholders and teams. Establish clear timelines, milestones, and accountability mechanisms to track progress.

- **Create a Roadmap**: Develop a comprehensive roadmap outlining the timeline and milestones for implementing the agreed-upon actions. Include resource allocation, budget considerations, and dependencies.

- **Review and Iterate**: Schedule regular reviews and checkpoints to monitor progress, evaluate effectiveness, and make necessary adjustments to the cloud security strategy. Continuously iterate and improve your organization's cloud security posture.

By conducting this exercise, business owners can gain valuable insights into their organization's current state of cloud security, identify key challenges, and develop actionable strategies to enhance security resilience and mitigate risks effectively.

Chapter 2

Striking the right balance among Cloud Network Security, Cost Management, and Generative AI Security

Ignoring cloud security in today's business landscape is akin to leaving your doors unlocked in a high-risk neighbourhood. Let's understand Cloud Network Security and its impact on business expansion, to not just lock your doors but to fortify them in the era of digital transformation.

In any business endeavour, the potential for profitability and growth is paramount. By carefully balancing these elements, businesses can create a harmonious environment where advanced security, cost efficiency, and innovative AI drive growth and resilience.

Requisite and Importance of Cloud and Cloud Network Security on Business Performance

The adoption of cloud computing has become a cornerstone for businesses seeking efficiency, scalability, and innovation. However, with the increasing reliance on cloud services, the importance of robust cloud security measures cannot be overstated for its transformative impact on modern businesses.

Importance of Cloud:

- **Scalability and Flexibility**: Cloud computing allows businesses to scale their IT resources up or down based on current needs. This flexibility is crucial for handling fluctuating workloads and supports business growth without the need for significant upfront investment in physical infrastructure.

- **Cost Efficiency**: With cloud computing, businesses can significantly reduce costs associated with purchasing, maintaining, and upgrading IT hardware and infrastructure. The pay-as-you-go model of cloud services means companies pay only for what they use, leading to more efficient budget management.

- **Accessibility and Collaboration**: The cloud enables data and applications to be accessed from anywhere, at any time, facilitating remote work and global collaboration. This accessibility improves productivity and allows teams to work together more efficiently, regardless of their location.

- **Disaster Recovery and Data Backup**: Cloud services provide robust solutions for data backup and disaster recovery. This is crucial for business continuity, ensuring that data is securely backed up and can be quickly restored in the event of data loss or a disaster.

- **Enhanced Security**: Reputable cloud service providers offer advanced security features that protect sensitive data from cyber threats. These features can include data encryption, intrusion detection, and regular security audits, which are often more robust than what a business could afford to implement on its own.

- **Compliance and Regulatory Adherence**: Cloud providers often ensure that their services are compliant with various regulatory standards, which can be beneficial for businesses that need to meet specific compliance requirements, such as GDPR, HIPAA, or PCI DSS.

- **Sustainability**: By using shared resources in the cloud, businesses can reduce their carbon footprint. Cloud data centres are typically more energy-efficient than traditional on-premise data centres, supporting corporate sustainability goals.

- **Innovation and Competitiveness**: The cloud offers access to the latest technologies, such as artificial intelligence, machine learning, and big data analytics, enabling businesses to innovate and stay competitive. This access allows companies to develop new products and services quickly and respond to market changes more effectively.

- **Focus on Core Business**: By outsourcing IT infrastructure to cloud providers, businesses can focus more on their core operations rather than being bogged down by IT management. This shift in focus can lead to improved productivity and business growth.

- **Global Reach**: Cloud computing enables businesses to easily deploy their services in multiple regions across the globe, helping them to expand their market reach and operate on a global scale without the need for physical presence.

Importance of Cloud Network Security:

- **Enhanced Data Security**: Strong cloud network security protects sensitive business and customer data from breaches, unauthorized access, and cyberattacks. This protection is crucial for maintaining the confidentiality and integrity of business data.

- **Compliance and Regulatory Adherence**: Businesses are often subject to various regulations regarding data protection and privacy. Robust cloud network security helps in complying with these regulations, avoiding legal penalties and fines.

- **Increased Customer Trust**: Customers are increasingly concerned about their data privacy. Demonstrating strong security practices helps in building and maintaining customer trust and loyalty.

- **Business Continuity and Resilience**: Effective security measures reduce the risk of disruptions caused by cyber threats, ensuring continuous business operations and minimizing potential downtime.

- **Competitive Advantage**: Businesses with strong cloud network security can leverage this as a competitive advantage, especially in industries where data security is a significant concern.

- **Cost Savings**: While implementing security measures requires investment, it can lead to cost savings in the long run by preventing costly breaches and maintaining operational efficiency.

- **Facilitation of Remote Work**: With secure cloud networks, businesses can safely offer remote work options, expanding their talent pool and enhancing employee satisfaction without compromising on data security.

- **Innovation and Agility**: Secure cloud environments enable businesses to confidently adopt new technologies and innovate, staying agile and responsive to market changes.

Cloud Security Investment: Boon for Business or Budgetary Burden?

In the digital age, cloud security is not an optional add-on; it's an essential pillar of a robust, resilient, and dynamic business model. Investing in cloud security is predominantly seen as a strategic and profitable investment rather than a loss, especially when considering the long-term benefits and protections it offers to a business. Some of the key points are:

- **Risk Mitigation**: The cost of a data breach can be substantial, not just in terms of financial loss but also in terms of damaged reputation and lost trust. Investing in cloud security significantly reduces these risks.

- **Regulatory Compliance**: Non-compliance with data protection regulations can lead to hefty fines. A secure cloud environment ensures compliance and avoids such financial penalties.

- **Business Continuity**: Cloud security safeguards against disruptions to operations, ensuring that businesses can continue to function effectively, even in the face of cyber threats.

- **Customer Trust**: In an era where customers are increasingly concerned about data privacy, demonstrating strong security practices is essential for maintaining customer trust and loyalty.

- **Competitive Advantage**: Companies that invest in cloud security can leverage this as a competitive advantage, especially in industries where data security is a significant concern.

- **Long-Term Savings**: While there is an upfront cost to implementing cloud security measures, the potential savings from avoiding data breaches, operational disruptions, and non-compliance fines can be substantial over time.

With cloud security in your arsenal, you're not just fortifying your defences; you're unlocking new horizons for your business. It's a journey towards a more secure, agile, and prosperous future, where your business is ready to face the challenges of the digital world and emerge stronger.

Case Study: Cloud Security Investment - Boon for Business or Budgetary Burden?

Having worked closely with a medium-sized e-commerce company, I've witnessed firsthand the dynamic landscape of cloud security investment. This company, amidst the rapid expansion of its online platform and customer base, made a significant move to the cloud to boost scalability, flexibility, and cost efficiency. However, this transition didn't come without its share of debates and concerns regarding the necessity and financial viability of investing in cloud security measures.

Here's what I observed:

Migration to the Cloud: The company opted to transition its operations to cloud service providers like Amazon Web Services (AWS) and Microsoft Azure to capitalize on the advantages of cloud computing. This move enabled them to cut infrastructure costs, enhance agility, and better scale their services to meet customer demands.

Security Concerns: Despite the benefits of cloud adoption, the company grappled with significant security concerns related to data breaches, unauthorized access, and compliance risks. Protecting sensitive customer data, intellectual property, and business-critical applications hosted in the cloud emerged as top priorities, albeit with challenges in justifying the investment in robust security measures.

Budget Constraints: Operating within a tight budget environment, the company's leadership hesitated to allocate additional funds for cloud security. There was apprehension that such investments might strain financial resources and impact profitability, leading to a perception that cloud security was a discretionary expense rather than a strategic imperative.

Regulatory Compliance: Operating in a heavily regulated industry, compliance with data protection and privacy regulations such as GDPR and PCI DSS was paramount.

Non-compliance could result in severe financial penalties, legal liabilities, and damage to the company's reputation, necessitating alignment of cloud security measures with regulatory standards.

Risk Management Strategy: While the company acknowledged the importance of a risk-based approach to cloud security, there was a lack of consensus on balancing security needs with budgetary constraints effectively.

Strategies Implemented:

Risk Assessment and Prioritization: Conducted a thorough risk assessment to identify and prioritize security risks associated with cloud adoption was essential. This helped justify investments in cloud security measures by evaluating potential impacts on business operations, customer trust, and regulatory compliance.

Cost-Benefit Analysis: Performed a cost-benefit analysis to quantify the financial, operational, and reputational impacts of security breaches versus the cost of implementing cloud security solutions was crucial for informed decision-making.

Security by Design: Incorporated security considerations into the design, development, and implementation of cloud-based systems and applications from the outset was imperative. This involved adopting security best practices such as encryption, multi-factor authentication, network segmentation, and intrusion detection.

Continuous Monitoring and Compliance: Implemented robust monitoring and compliance mechanisms to track and audit cloud infrastructure, services, and user activities in real time was necessary. Leveraging cloud-native security tools and third-party solutions helped detect and respond to security incidents promptly while maintaining visibility into cloud environments.

Investment in Training and Talent: Invested in employee training and skill development programs to enhance cybersecurity awareness, expertise, and proficiency within the organization was vital. This empowered employees to recognize security threats, adhere to security policies and procedures, and contribute to a culture of proactive risk management and incident response.

By adopting a proactive and strategic approach to cloud security investment, the company mitigated security risks, enhanced regulatory compliance, and strengthened its competitive advantage in the digital marketplace. Instead of viewing cloud security as a budgetary burden, the organization leveraged it as a strategic enabler for business growth, innovation, and customer trust in an increasingly interconnected and data-driven world.

Requisite of Cost Optimisation and its Technique

How to achieve cost savings through the optimization of cloud resources and the implementation of efficient security measures. How to position the company as an industry leader with a strong focus on cybersecurity. By carefully considering some factors, businesses can ensure they are investing wisely in cloud network security, obtaining the necessary level of protection without unnecessary expenditure.

- **Assess Your Specific Security Needs**: Conduct a thorough assessment of your unique security requirements. Avoid overspending on unnecessary features by tailoring the security measures to your actual risk profile and business needs.

- **Choose Scalable Solutions**: Opt for cloud security solutions that offer scalability. This way, you can start with what you need and scale up as your business grows, ensuring you only pay for the resources you use.

- **Compare Different Providers**: Shop around and compare the offerings and pricing of different cloud security providers. Look for competitive pricing but also consider the reputation, reliability, and the range of services offered.

- **Utilize Integrated Security Suites**: Integrated security solutions, which offer a range of tools in a single package, can be more cost-effective than purchasing separate products for each security need.

- **Consider Open-Source Tools**: Explore open-source security tools, which can be less expensive than commercial products. Ensure they are reliable and have strong community support.

- **Prioritize Multi-Layered Security**: Implement a multi-layered security approach that includes essential elements like firewalls, intrusion detection systems, and encryption. This layered defence can prevent costly security breaches.

- **Opt for Managed Security Services**: If in-house expertise is limited, consider managed security services. These can be more cost-effective than building an in-house team, especially for small to medium-sized businesses.

- **Regularly Review and Adjust Your Security Strategy**: Continuously monitor and review your cloud security measures. Adjust your strategy as needed to address emerging threats and eliminate redundant or ineffective tools.

- **Train Your Staff in Security Best Practices**: Invest in training your employees on security best practices. Human error can lead to security breaches, and educated staff are your first line of defence.

- **Leverage Automation**: Use automation in security monitoring and response where possible. Automation can reduce the manpower needed and improve response times to threats.

- **Understand the Shared Responsibility Model**: In cloud computing, security is often a shared responsibility between the provider and the user. Understand your responsibilities and leverage the security controls provided by the cloud service provider.

Requisite and overview of AI-based Cloud Security to make business future-ready and cost-efficient

The Role of AI in Threat Detection and Prevention: AI's prowess in pattern recognition and anomaly detection revolutionizes threat detection in cloud environments. AI algorithms can analyse vast datasets in real time, identify potential threats, and proactively prevent security breaches.

The integration of AI enhances the speed and accuracy of security responses.

Automated Incident Response: Accelerating Mitigation Efforts: AI empowers automated incident response, minimizing the response time to security events. AI-driven systems can autonomously identify and mitigate security incidents, reducing the manual workload for security teams and enhancing the overall responsiveness of cloud security protocols.

Predictive Analytics for Resource Scaling and Optimization: AI's predictive analytics capabilities extend to resource scaling in the cloud. AI algorithms can analyse historical usage patterns, predict future resource needs, and dynamically scale resources. This not only optimizes costs but also ensures that businesses are equipped to handle varying workloads effectively.

AI-Enhanced Encryption and Data Privacy Measures: The security of sensitive data is paramount, and AI plays a crucial role in enhancing encryption and data privacy measures. AI-driven encryption algorithms can adapt to evolving threats, providing a dynamic defence against unauthorized access and ensuring the privacy of critical information.

Real-time Monitoring and Adaptive Security Measures: AI enables real-time monitoring of cloud environments, allowing for adaptive security measures. AI continuously analyses network activities, identifies anomalies, and adjusts security protocols in real time. This proactive approach enhances the resilience of cloud security against emerging threats.

AI-Driven Compliance Management and Reporting:
Compliance with regulatory standards is a complex but
necessary aspect of business operations. AI streamlines
compliance management by automating tasks such as audit
preparation, monitoring changes in regulations, and ensuring
adherence to data protection laws. AI-driven compliance
management contributes to both security and cost efficiency.

Cost Optimization through AI-Generated Insights: AI-
generated insights play a pivotal role in optimizing costs in
cloud security. AI can analyse cost-related data, identify
areas of inefficiency, and recommend adjustments to
resource allocation. The synergy between AI and cost
management contributes to a lean and efficient cloud security
infrastructure.

Business Intelligence and Decision Support: Beyond
security and cost management, AI provides valuable business
intelligence. AI-driven analytics can offer insights into user
behaviour, trends, and potential areas for business growth.
By leveraging AI for decision support, organizations can
make informed choices that align with both security and
business objectives.

The Triad of Success: Mastering Cloud Networking Security, Generative AI Security Integration, and Cost Management for Profit

The balance of cloud networking, Generative AI security, and
cost management is a guiding star in this digital voyage,
steering businesses towards a horizon filled with innovation,
security, and sustainable growth. Maintaining a balance
between Cloud Networking, Generative AI security, and Cost
Management can significantly profit a business in various
ways:

- **Enhanced Operational Efficiency**: Integrating cloud networking and Generative AI security optimizes business operations. AI can automate routine tasks and analyse large data sets, leading to quicker decision-making and increased productivity.

- **Cost-Effective Innovation**: By balancing these elements, businesses can innovate without incurring excessive costs. Cloud networking offers scalable solutions, while Generative AI security provides cost-effective ways to enhance products and services.

- **Improved Security and Risk Management**: Cloud network security protects valuable data and assets. Generative AI security can enhance this by predicting and mitigating potential threats, leading to a more secure business environment.

- **Data-Driven Insights**: Generative AI security can analyse cloud-based data to uncover insights that can drive business strategy and operational improvements, offering a competitive advantage in the market.

- **Better Resource Allocation**: Effective cost management ensures that resources are allocated optimally. Investments in cloud networking and Generative AI security are made strategically, ensuring maximum return on investment.

- **Increased Scalability and Flexibility**: Cloud networking provides the flexibility to scale operations up or down as needed, which, when coupled with Generative AI security, allows businesses to adapt quickly to market changes or operational demands.

- **Enhanced Customer Experiences**: Generative AI security can personalize customer experiences, while cloud networking ensures seamless service delivery. This combination can lead to higher customer satisfaction and loyalty.

- **Streamlined Compliance and Governance**: Cloud solutions can help streamline compliance with various regulations. Generative AI security can assist in monitoring and maintaining these compliance standards, reducing the risk of costly legal issues.

- **Long-Term Financial Health**: By managing costs effectively while investing in cloud and Generative AI technologies, businesses can ensure long-term financial stability and growth.

- **Innovation and Market Positioning**: Balancing these elements positions a business as a forward-thinking leader, capable of leveraging the latest technologies to stay ahead in the market.

By striking the right balance between cloud network, generative AI security and cost, you will not only safeguard your business's present but also unlock its future potential, paving the way for enduring success in an ever-evolving digital world.

Case Study: The Triad of Success: Mastering Cloud Networking Security, Generative AI Security Integration, and Cost Management for Profit

Having collaborated closely with a global technology company specializing in data analytics solutions, I've seen firsthand the strategic importance of mastering cloud networking security, generative AI security integration, and cost management to drive profitability and success in a fiercely competitive market landscape.

Here's what I observed:

Cloud Networking Security: As the company migrates its infrastructure and applications to the cloud, ensuring robust network security becomes paramount. Challenges arise related to data protection, network segmentation, access control, and compliance in a distributed cloud environment.

Generative AI Security Integration: Leveraging generative AI algorithms to analyze large datasets and derive actionable insights introduces new security risks related to data privacy, model vulnerabilities, adversarial attacks, and ethical considerations.

Cost Management for Profit: Optimizing cloud costs while maximizing profitability and operational efficiency presents a balancing act. The company must balance scalability and performance with cost-effective resource allocation, utilization monitoring, and optimization strategies.

Strategies Implemented:

Cloud Networking Security: Adopted a defence-in-depth approach, the company leverages network segmentation, encryption, identity and access management (IAM), and threat detection and response mechanisms. Regular security audits, vulnerability assessments, and compliance checks helped maintain a proactive stance against emerging threats and regulatory requirements.

Generative AI Security Integration: Established a dedicated AI security team responsible for assessing, monitoring, and mitigating risks associated with generative AI algorithms and models. Robust data governance policies, encryption protocols, and access controls protected sensitive data used in AI training and inference processes. Investment in AI-specific security tools and technologies helped detect and mitigate adversarial attacks and other AI-specific threats.

Cost Management for Profit: Leveraged cloud cost management tools and services to track, analyze, and optimize cloud spending across multiple environments and workloads. Implemented automation scripts, resource tagging, and budget alerts enforced cost controls, prevented resource sprawl, and identified optimization opportunities. Continuous evaluation of cloud architecture, workload performance, and pricing options aligned resource allocation with business priorities and cost-saving initiatives.

Results and Benefits:

Enhanced Security Posture: By mastering cloud networking security and generative AI security integration, the company strengthened its overall security posture, mitigated cyber threats, and built trust with customers and stakeholders.

Optimized Cost Management: Proactive cost management strategies and optimization initiatives result in significant cost savings, improved resource utilization, and maximized return on investment (ROI) by 75% in cloud infrastructure and AI capabilities.

Sustainable Profitability: The successful integration of cloud networking security, generative AI security, and cost management practices enabled the company to drive sustainable profitability, innovation, and growth in the rapidly evolving technology landscape.

By prioritizing the triad of cloud networking security, generative AI security integration, and cost management for profit, the company positioned itself as a leader in delivering secure, scalable, and cost-effective data analytics solutions to its global clientele.

Financial Analysis for Investing in Cloud Security

Steps for Profit Calculation

Calculating the profit earned by using various security tools such as Generative AI tools, Firewalls, Antivirus software, and CISM (Certified Information Security Manager) tools involves assessing the impact of these tools on the organization's overall security posture, operational efficiency, and financial performance. Here are some steps you can follow to estimate the profit earned:

- **Define Key Performance Indicators (KPIs)**: Identify the key metrics and performance indicators that are relevant to your organization's security goals and objectives. These could include metrics such as reduction in security incidents, time saved in incident response, increased productivity due to improved security, and cost savings from mitigating security breaches.

- **Assess Cost of Security Tools**: Calculate the total cost associated with acquiring, implementing, and maintaining the security tools, including licensing fees, hardware costs, personnel training, and ongoing support and maintenance expenses.

- **Quantify Security Improvements**: Evaluate the impact of the security tools on your organization's security posture. Measure the reduction in security incidents, such as malware infections, data breaches, unauthorized access attempts, and other security breaches, attributable to the deployment of these tools.

- **Estimate Time and Resource Savings**: Determine the amount of time and resources saved by using the security tools. This could include time saved by automated threat detection and response mechanisms, reduced manual effort in security management tasks, and improved operational efficiency due to enhanced security controls.

- **Calculate Cost Avoidance and ROI**: Compare the cost of implementing and maintaining the security tools with the financial benefits derived from improved security and operational efficiency. Calculate the cost avoidance achieved by mitigating security incidents and the return on investment (ROI) by dividing the net financial benefits (total savings minus total costs) by the total cost of investment, expressed as a percentage.

- **Consider Intangible Benefits**: In addition to quantifiable financial benefits, consider the intangible benefits associated with enhanced security, such as improved customer trust and loyalty, enhanced brand reputation, and reduced business risk exposure.

- **Periodic Review and Adjustment**: Continuously monitor and assess the performance and effectiveness of the security tools over time. Periodically review and adjust your security strategy and toolset to adapt to evolving threats and changing business requirements.

These steps can develop a comprehensive understanding of the profit earned by using security tools and justify the investment in cybersecurity measures to stakeholders within your organization.

General guidelines for recording entries on the Balance Sheet

Adding the costs and profits earned from using various tools such as Generative AI tools, Firewalls, Antivirus software, CISM (Certified Information Security Manager) tools, and others to a balance sheet involves proper accounting practices. Here's a general guideline:

- **Identify Costs**: First, identify the costs associated with acquiring and using these tools. This includes initial purchase costs, subscription fees, licensing fees, maintenance costs, and any other related expenses. These costs should be recorded as expenses on the income statement during the period they are incurred.

- **Amortization or Depreciation**: Depending on the nature of the tools and their expected useful life, you may need to amortize or depreciate the costs over time. Amortization is typically used for intangible assets like software licenses, while depreciation is used for tangible assets like hardware appliances. The amortization or depreciation expense should be recorded on the income statement and accumulated on the balance sheet under the respective asset accounts.

- **Track Revenue or Savings**: Determine how these tools contribute to revenue generation or cost savings for the business. For example, if the use of security tools reduces the risk of cyberattacks and potential financial losses, it contributes to cost savings. If the tools enable the business to offer enhanced security services to clients, it may lead to increased revenue.

- **Record Revenue or Savings**: Revenue generated or cost savings achieved through the use of these tools should be recorded on the income statement as appropriate. For example, if the company provides cybersecurity services to clients, the revenue generated from these services would be recorded as income. Similarly, cost savings resulting from reduced cybersecurity incidents would contribute to the company's profitability.

- **Update Balance Sheet**: The net impact of the costs and revenues/savings associated with these tools will ultimately affect the company's overall financial position. The net result should be reflected in the balance sheet through changes in asset and liability accounts, such as cash, accounts receivable, prepaid expenses, or accrued liabilities, depending on the specific transactions and timing of the financial reporting period.

These guidelines can help reflect the costs and benefits of using security tools on your company's balance sheet and financial statements after consulting a financial advisor.

Example Balance Sheet and Return on Investment (ROI) Computation

Creating a balance sheet involves detailing a company's financial position at a specific point in time. I providing a simplified example based on the assumption of costs and profits earned from using various cybersecurity tools such as generative AI tools, firewalls, antivirus software, and Cloud Security Posture Management tools.

Assumptions:

Cost of cybersecurity tools: $100,000

Profit earned through enhanced security services: $200,000

Balance Sheet

Assets in Dollars		Liability and Equity in Dollars	
Cash *(Current Assets)*	100,000	Accounts Payable *(Current Liability)*	20,000
Accounts Receivable *(Current Assets)*	50,000	Short-term Loans *(Current Liability)*	30,000
Inventory *(Current Assets)*	0	Accrued Expenses *(Current Liability)*	10,000
Prepaid Expenses *(Current Assets)*	10,000	Long-term Loans *(Non-Current Liability)*	50,000
Property, Plant, and Equipment	50,000	Capital Stock *(Equity)*	100,000

(non-Current Assets)			
Intangible Assets (Cybersecurity Tools) *(non-Current Assets)*	100,000	Retained Earnings *(Equity)*	100,000
	310,000		**310,000**

Asset = Liabilities + Equity = $310,000

This is a simplified example so it is important to consult with a financial expert or accountant to create a balance sheet tailored to your company's financial data and requirements.

ROI calculation

Based on the assumption in the above example

Assumptions:

- Cost of cybersecurity tools: $100,000

- Profit earned through enhanced security services: $200,000

Using the ROI formula:

ROI = (Net Profit/Cost of Investment) × 100%

Given:

- Net Profit = $200,000 (profit earned)

- Cost of Investment = $100,000 (cost of cybersecurity tools)

Substitute the values into the formula:

ROI = (200,000/100,000) × 100%

ROI = (2) × 100%

ROI = 200%

The ROI for the investment in cybersecurity tools is 200%. This means that for every dollar invested in cybersecurity tools, the company earned a profit of $2.00.

Summary:

The Triad of Success: Mastering Cloud Networking Security, Generative AI security Integration, and Cost Management for Profit

- *Why is the migration to the cloud and the implementation of defense-in-depth through Zero Trust methodology significant?*

- *What drives the necessity for cost optimization in the digital realm, and what methodologies exist to optimize expenses?*

- *In what ways does the integration of AI into Cloud Security become imperative for businesses to ensure future readiness and cost-effectiveness?*

- *How essential are cloud network security, Generative AI, and cost management for fostering business growth and profitability?*

Exercise:

Objective: To develop a comprehensive strategy for mastering cloud networking security, generative AI security integration, and cost management to drive profitability and success in your organization.

Steps:

Assessment of Current State:

- Evaluate your organization's current practices and capabilities in cloud networking security, generative AI security integration, and cost management.

- Identify strengths, weaknesses, opportunities, and threats related to each component of the triad.

Define Business Objectives:

- Clarify your organization's business objectives and priorities related to security, innovation, cost optimization, and profitability.

- Determine how mastering cloud networking security, generative AI security integration, and cost management align with your overarching business goals.

Cloud Networking Security:

- Identify critical assets, data repositories, and network infrastructure components that require protection in your cloud environment.

Develop a comprehensive security strategy encompassing network segmentation, encryption, identity and access management (IAM), threat detection, and incident response.

- Establish policies and procedures for security compliance, audit trails, and regulatory requirements applicable to your industry.

Generative AI Security Integration:

- Assess the security implications of deploying generative AI algorithms and models within your organization.

- Implement measures to secure data used in AI training and inference processes, including data encryption, access controls, and anonymization techniques.

- Incorporate AI-specific security tools and technologies to detect and mitigate adversarial attacks, model vulnerabilities, and data privacy risks.

Cost Management for Profit:

- Analyze your organization's cloud spending patterns, resource utilization, and cost drivers across different cloud services and environments.

- Implement cost optimization strategies such as rightsizing instances, leveraging reserved capacity, utilizing spot instances, and implementing auto-scaling policies.

- Monitor and track cloud costs using cost management tools and services to identify opportunities for cost savings and efficiency improvements.

Integration and Synergy:

- Identify areas of synergy and integration between cloud networking security, generative AI security integration, and cost management initiatives.

- Explore how improvements in one area can positively impact the others, such as implementing cost-effective security measures or leveraging AI-driven insights for cost optimization.

- Foster collaboration and communication between teams responsible for each component of the triad to ensure alignment with overall business objectives.

Training and Awareness:

- Provide training and awareness programs for employees, stakeholders, and partners on the importance of cloud networking security, generative AI security integration, and cost management best practices.

- Encourage a culture of security awareness, innovation, and cost-consciousness throughout the organization.

Continuous Improvement:

- Establish metrics, key performance indicators (KPIs), and benchmarks to measure the effectiveness of your initiatives in mastering the triad of success.

- Conduct regular reviews, audits, and assessments to identify areas for improvement and adaptation to evolving security threats, technological advancements, and business requirements.

Conclusion: By mastering cloud networking security, generative AI security integration, and cost management for profit, organizations can enhance their competitive advantage, drive innovation, and achieve sustainable growth in the dynamic digital landscape. This exercise provides a structured approach to develop and implement a holistic strategy that aligns with your organization's business objectives and priorities.

Chapter 3

Cost efficient Cloud Network Security Components

How much could your business transform if you mastered the art of balancing world-class security with cost-effective strategies in the cloud? Some of the cost-efficient cloud network security components empowered by AI helped in strategic decisions in today's fast-paced digital marketplace for enhanced business security.

Implementing Cost-Effective Robust Strategies in the Cloud

By incorporating some simple strategies, businesses can significantly strengthen their cloud network security, protecting themselves against cyber threats and ensuring the safety of their data and operations. Adopting cost-effective strategies for implementing network security like Firewalls, NSG/ASG rules, Routing, and Policies are crucial for maintaining both security and budgetary health in cloud computing environments. To enhance and tighten security around cloud networking, businesses several key strategies:

- **Strong Authentication Protocols**: Implement multi-factor authentication (MFA) to add an extra layer of security beyond just passwords. This can include biometrics, one-time passcodes, or security tokens. MFA acts as a deterrent against unauthorized access attempts, reducing the likelihood of successful account takeovers.

The prevention of such incidents contributes to the overall cost-effectiveness of MFA implementation.

- **Advanced Encryption Techniques**: Use strong encryption for data at rest and in transit. This ensures that even if data is intercepted or accessed, it remains unreadable and secure. Encryption helps organizations comply with data protection regulations, reducing the risk of legal consequences and potential financial penalties associated with non-compliance.

- **Regular Security Audits and Compliance Checks**: Conduct periodic security audits to identify vulnerabilities. Ensure compliance with industry standards and regulations to maintain high security levels. Regular security audits and compliance checks are cost-effective by minimising the financial impact of potential breaches, avoiding non-compliance penalties, and fostering a secure environment, ultimately saving resources and safeguarding the organization's financial well-being.

- **Employ Intrusion Detection and Prevention Systems**: Utilize systems that can detect and prevent unauthorized access or anomalies in network traffic, providing real-time security against potential breaches. By preventing unauthorized access and mitigating potential damages, IDPS reduces incident response costs, safeguards critical assets, and ensures business continuity.

- **Access Control and User Permissions**: Implement strict access control policies. Define user roles and permissions clearly to ensure that only authorized personnel have access to sensitive data and operations.

This minimizes the risk of data breaches, internal threats, and unauthorized activities. organizations avoid potential financial losses associated with data compromise, legal consequences, and reputational damage, ensuring robust protection within budget constraints.

- **Continuous Monitoring and Real-Time Alerts**: Monitor cloud networks continuously for unusual activities. Set up real-time alerts to notify administrators of potential security threats. Continuous monitoring and real-time alerts are cost-effective by providing swift detection of security incidents. This proactive approach minimizes the impact and costs associated with data breaches, allowing organizations to respond promptly.

- **Employee Training and Awareness Programs**: Regularly train employees on security best practices, phishing awareness, and the importance of maintaining data confidentiality. Employee training and awareness programs are cost-effective by reducing the risk of human errors and security incidents. Well-informed employees are less likely to fall victim to phishing or social engineering attacks, mitigating the potential financial impact of data breaches.

- **Backup and Disaster Recovery Plans**: Develop and maintain robust data backup and disaster recovery plans to ensure business continuity in the event of a data breach or loss. Backup and disaster recovery plans are cost-effective by mitigating potential financial losses in the event of data loss or system failures. Timely recovery minimizes downtime, preventing revenue loss, reputational damage, and operational disruptions, thus reducing the overall cost of recovery.

- **Secure Endpoints and Mobile Devices**: Secure all endpoints, including employee devices that access the cloud network, with appropriate security software and regular updates. Robust endpoint security reduces the risk of malware infections and unauthorized access, minimizing incident response costs and avoiding financial losses associated with compromised devices.

- **Implement Cloud Security Posture Management (CSPM)**: Use CSPM tools to automatically identify and remediate risks across cloud infrastructures, improving overall security posture. CSPM identifies misconfigurations and vulnerabilities, preventing potential breaches and data leaks. Proactive security measures reduce the financial impact of incidents, safeguarding assets and minimizing the costs associated with remediation and recovery.

- **Partner with Reputable Cloud Providers**: Choose cloud service providers with strong security track records. Evaluate their security policies, practices, and infrastructure. Their established infrastructure often results in improved reliability, minimizing downtime costs.

- **Zero Trust Security Model**: Adopt a zero-trust approach where trust is never assumed, and verification is required from everyone trying to access resources in your network. The Zero Trust Security Model is cost-effective by minimizing the impact of security incidents. Its principle of continuous verification and strict access controls reduces the risk of data breaches and unauthorized access

- **Advanced Firewalls**: Deploy state-of-the-art firewalls that offer comprehensive protection against a wide range of cyber threats. These firewalls should be capable of inspecting incoming and outgoing traffic, blocking malicious traffic, and preventing unauthorized access.
To optimize Firewall Deployment, choose firewalls that offer the best balance between cost and functionality. Consider cloud-native firewalls in a single cloud environment, which might offer more cost-effective solutions compared to traditional hardware-based firewalls. Firewalls are cost-effective by preventing unauthorized access, protecting against cyber threats, and reducing the risk of data breaches. This proactive defence helps avoid financial losses, including those associated with incident response and data recovery.

- **Network Security Group (NSG) and Application Security Group (ASG) Rules:** Utilize NSGs and ASGs to control inbound and outbound network traffic to and from cloud resources. These rules help in segmenting network traffic, ensuring that only legitimate traffic is allowed. Utilize Network Security Groups (NSG) and Application Security Groups (ASG) effectively by creating targeted rules that protect your network without over-complicating your security infrastructure. This strategic implementation helps in avoiding unnecessary costs associated with managing overly complex rules. Network Security Group (NSG) and Application Security Group (ASG) rules are cost-effective by providing granular control over network traffic. These rules allow organizations to define specific access policies, reducing the risk of unauthorized access and potential security incidents.

- **Effective Routing**: Implement secure and efficient routing mechanisms. This includes the use of Virtual Private Networks (VPNs) and secure routing protocols to ensure that data travels through safe and controlled pathways. Implement routing protocols that are both secure and efficient. Opt for solutions that provide optimal network performance with minimal resource usage to reduce costs associated with data transfer and network management.

- **Whitelisting**: Adopt a whitelisting approach where only pre-approved applications, IP addresses, or domains are allowed access to your network. This minimizes the risk of malicious entities gaining access.

- **Strict Policy Enforcement**: Develop and enforce robust security policies across the organization. This includes policies for data handling, user authentication, device usage, and incident response. Develop security policies that are both robust and cost-effective. Avoid overly restrictive policies that can incur additional costs in terms of system resources and administrative overhead.

Leveraging cost-efficient robust Antivirus software and Extended Detection and Response (XDR) solutions

Advanced Antivirus Software offers comprehensive protection against malware, viruses, spyware, and other malicious software. Extended Detection and Response (XDR) Solutions provide an integrated and comprehensive approach to threat detection and response across various layers of the network, including email, endpoints, servers, cloud workloads, and networks. To achieve a balance between cost-efficiency and robustness in Antivirus and Extended Detection and Response (XDR) solutions, consider the following strategies:

- **Evaluate Total Cost of Ownership:** Look beyond just the initial purchase price. Consider the long-term costs associated with maintenance, updates, and support for the antivirus and XDR solutions.

- **Choose Scalable Solutions**: Opt for antivirus and XDR solutions that can scale with your business needs. This avoids the need for costly upgrades or replacements as your business grows or your security needs change.

- **Prioritize Essential Features**: Identify the key features that are essential for your organization's security. Focus on solutions that provide these core functionalities without unnecessary extras that add to the cost.

- **Consider Cloud-Based Services**: Cloud-based antivirus and XDR solutions can be more cost-effective than on-premise solutions, as they often require less hardware investment and reduced maintenance costs.

- **Leverage AI and Automation**: Solutions that incorporate artificial intelligence and automation can enhance threat detection and response capabilities while also reducing the need for manual intervention, thus saving on labour costs.

- **Seek Bundled or Integrated Solutions**: Look for providers that offer bundled security solutions or platforms that integrate antivirus and XDR functionalities. Bundled pricing can often be more cost-effective than purchasing separate products.

- **Negotiate with Vendors**: Don't hesitate to negotiate pricing with vendors based on your specific needs and budget constraints. Vendors are often willing to work with clients to find a suitable pricing model.

- **Stay Informed About New Developments**: The cybersecurity field is rapidly evolving. Stay informed about the latest developments in antivirus and XDR solutions to take advantage of new, more efficient, and potentially more cost-effective technologies.

- **Regularly Review and Assess Needs**: Continuously assess your cybersecurity needs and the performance of your chosen solutions. This helps ensure that you are not overpaying for unnecessary features or under-protected by outdated technology.

By carefully selecting and managing antivirus and XDR solutions, businesses can ensure robust cybersecurity protection while maintaining cost efficiency.

Streamlining Monitoring, Reviewing, and Auditing processes for Cost-effectiveness

Vigilant Monitoring involves real-time surveillance to detect unusual behaviour or anomalies that could indicate a security threat, ensuring immediate action can be taken. Regular Reviewing includes assessing user access levels, examining security settings, and updating protocols to address new threats. Thorough Auditing covers compliance with industry standards, data protection laws, and internal security policies. Audits help in identifying potential vulnerabilities and gaps in your security framework. Streamlining monitoring, reviewing, and auditing processes for cost-effectiveness involves creating a more efficient and resource-effective approach to these critical security practices:

- **Automated Monitoring Tools**: Implement automated tools for continuous monitoring of your network and systems. Automation can help detect anomalies, reduce manual labour, and increase efficiency, leading to cost savings.

- **Regular, Scheduled Reviews**: Establish a regular schedule for reviewing security policies and configurations. This consistent approach ensures nothing is overlooked and can be more cost-effective than ad-hoc reviews, which may require additional resources.

- **Integrated Auditing Platforms**: Utilize integrated platforms that can consolidate auditing processes across various systems and applications. This consolidation can provide a comprehensive view of your security posture and reduce the resources needed for separate audits.

- **Risk-Based Auditing**: Adopt a risk-based approach to auditing by focusing on areas with the highest risk or potential impact. This prioritization ensures that resources are allocated effectively, addressing the most critical areas first.

- **Leveraging Cloud-Based Services**: Consider cloud-based monitoring and auditing services that can offer scalable and cost-effective solutions compared to in-house systems.

- **Data Analytics and AI**: Use data analytics and AI technologies to analyze large volumes of audit and monitoring data. These technologies can uncover insights more efficiently than manual analysis.

- **Streamlined Reporting**: Develop streamlined reporting processes to quickly and accurately convey findings from reviews and audits. Efficient reporting saves time and allows for faster decision-making.

- **Employee Training**: Train employees in best practices for monitoring and auditing. A well-informed team can carry out these processes more effectively and identify potential areas of cost savings.

- **Outsourcing Where Appropriate**: Consider outsourcing certain monitoring and auditing functions to specialized firms when it is more cost-effective than maintaining in-house capabilities.

- **Continuous Improvement**: Regularly assess the effectiveness of your monitoring, reviewing, and auditing processes. Look for ways to improve and streamline these operations to enhance efficiency and reduce costs over time.

By optimizing these processes, organizations can not only ensure thorough and effective security oversight but also manage these operations in a more cost-efficient manner.

Ensuring efficient resource utilization in Cloud Security Posture Management

Cloud Security Posture Management (CSPM) involves the use of automated tools and practices to continuously monitor and manage the security posture of cloud environments. This includes identifying misconfigurations, compliance violations, and potential security risks. Ensuring efficient resource utilization in Cloud Security Posture Management (CSPM) involves strategically leveraging resources to maximize security effectiveness while minimizing costs:

- **Automated Compliance Monitoring**: Use automated tools to continuously monitor compliance with security standards. This reduces the need for manual checks, saving time and manpower.

- **Targeted Resource Allocation**: Focus resources on the most critical areas of your cloud environment. Prioritize assets based on sensitivity and risk level to ensure high-value assets receive the most attention.

- **Integrating CSPM with Existing Tools**: Integrate CSPM solutions with existing security tools to create a unified security environment. This helps in resource optimization and eliminates the need for redundant tools.

- **Cloud-Native Solutions**: Employ cloud-native CSPM solutions that are designed specifically for cloud environments. These solutions can be more efficient and cost-effective compared to traditional security tools that may not be fully compatible with cloud architectures.

- **Regular Review of Security Posture**: Conduct regular reviews of your security posture to identify and eliminate redundant or unnecessary security measures, which can free up resources.

- **Scalable CSPM Solutions**: Choose CSPM solutions that can scale with your business needs. This flexibility allows you to adjust your security posture as your cloud environment grows or changes, ensuring you're not paying for unnecessary capabilities.

- **Data-Driven Decision Making**: Utilize data analytics within CSPM to make informed decisions about where to allocate resources. Analysing security data can help identify trends and areas that require more or less focus.

- **Employee Training and Awareness**: Train staff in efficient CSPM practices and the importance of resource management. An informed team can better maintain a secure cloud environment while optimizing resource use.

- **Outsourcing CSPM Functions**: Consider outsourcing certain CSPM functions to specialized service providers if it's more cost-effective than handling them in-house.

- **Leveraging AI and Machine Learning**: Utilize AI and machine learning algorithms within CSPM tools to automate routine tasks and provide predictive insights, which can help optimize resource usage.

By focusing on these areas, businesses can ensure that their CSPM strategy is not only effective in maintaining a strong cloud security posture but also efficient in terms of resource utilization, and balancing security needs with budgetary constraints.

Implementing access and privileged management solutions with a focus on cost optimization:

Implementing access and privileged management solutions while focusing on cost optimization involves strategically balancing security needs with financial efficiency:

- **Role-Based Access Control (RBAC)**: Utilize RBAC to assign permissions based on job roles. This efficient approach minimizes unnecessary access, reducing the risk of breaches while keeping the management straightforward and cost-effective.

- **Leverage Existing Identity Providers**: Integrate with existing identity management solutions (like Active Directory) to manage access rights. This can save costs on additional software and streamline the management process.

- **Automated Provisioning and Deprovisioning**: Automate the process of granting and revoking access rights to ensure timely updates to access privileges, reducing the administrative burden and associated costs.

- **Prioritize Critical Assets for Privileged Access Management (PAM)**: Focus PAM efforts on your most critical assets to get the most value from your investment. This means protecting the most sensitive systems and data first.

- **Use Open-Source or Cloud-Based PAM Solutions**: Consider open-source or cloud-based PAM solutions, which can be more cost-effective than traditional on-premises solutions.

- **Regular Access Reviews**: Conduct regular reviews of access rights to ensure that they are still necessary and appropriate. This helps in avoiding the accumulation of unnecessary access rights, which can pose security risks and administrative overhead.

- **Minimal Privilege Policy**: Implement the principle of least privilege, granting users only the access necessary for their role. This reduces the potential for internal threats and can simplify access management.

- **Monitor and Audit Privileged Activities**: Implement monitoring and auditing of privileged user activities to detect and respond to irregularities. Efficient auditing can be cost-effective by focusing on high-risk activities and automating audit processes.

- **Employee Training and Awareness**: Train employees on the importance of access control and the risks associated with privileged accounts. Well-informed employees are less likely to make costly security mistakes.

- **Evaluate and Adjust Regularly**: Continually assess the effectiveness and efficiency of your access and privileged management solutions. Adapt your strategies as your organization and security landscape evolve.

By focusing on these areas, organizations can effectively manage access and privileges in a way that maximizes security while also being mindful of budget constraints.

Balancing the effectiveness and costs of vulnerability management, particularly in Zero-Day threat protection

Balancing the effectiveness and costs of vulnerability management, especially in protecting against Zero-Day threats with AI tools, requires a strategic approach that aligns advanced security measures with budget considerations:

- **Prioritize Based on Risk Assessment**: Conduct thorough risk assessments to prioritize vulnerabilities, focusing resources on addressing the most critical threats first, including potential Zero-Day vulnerabilities.

- **AI-Driven Threat Intelligence**: Utilize AI-powered threat intelligence tools to identify and analyze emerging threats efficiently. AI can process vast amounts of data to detect patterns indicative of Zero-Day threats, providing cost-effective, proactive protection.

- **Automated Vulnerability Scanning**: Implement automated scanning tools that can continuously monitor for vulnerabilities. Automation increases efficiency and reduces the labour costs associated with manual scanning.

- **Cost-Benefit Analysis of Tools and Solutions**: Regularly perform cost-benefit analyses to ensure that the chosen AI tools and vulnerability management solutions provide optimal value and protection for their cost.

- **Integrate with Existing Security Infrastructure**: Seamlessly integrate AI tools with your existing security infrastructure to enhance capabilities without the need for entirely new systems, which can be more cost-effective.

- **Use of Open-Source Tools**: Where appropriate, incorporate open-source vulnerability management tools, which can be less expensive than proprietary solutions, while still offering robust protection.

- **Scalable Security Solutions**: Opt for scalable security solutions that can grow with your organization, ensuring that you are not paying for excessive capacity or features you do not need.

- **Regular Updates and Patches**: Maintain an efficient process for regular software updates and patch management, which is crucial for protecting against Zero-Day threats.

- **Employee Training and Awareness**: Educate staff about the latest threats and best practices for security. A well-informed team can be your first line of defence, helping to prevent expensive breaches.

- **Outsourcing to Specialized Providers**: Consider outsourcing certain aspects of vulnerability management to specialized providers, which can be more cost-effective than maintaining all capabilities in-house.

By focusing on these strategies, businesses can effectively manage the balance between cost and effectiveness in their vulnerability management practices, ensuring robust protection against advanced threats, including Zero-Day vulnerabilities, in a cost-conscious manner.

Adopting cost-effective measures for the operation and management of the Security Operations Center (SOC):

The SOC acts as a centralized unit that houses cybersecurity experts and analysts. This team is responsible for managing, monitoring, and analyzing security on an enterprise level. Adopting cost-effective measures for operating and managing a Security Operations Center (SOC) involves strategic planning and resource optimization to ensure high efficiency without compromising security effectiveness:

- **Leverage Automation and Orchestration**: Utilize automation tools to handle repetitive tasks and orchestration platforms to streamline response processes. This reduces manual labor and speeds up response times, making the SOC more efficient and cost-effective.

- **Outsourcing or Co-Managed SOCs**: Consider outsourcing your SOC or adopting a co-managed model. This can provide access to high-level expertise and advanced tools at a fraction of the cost of building and staffing a full in-house SOC.

- **Prioritize Critical Alerts**: Use intelligent systems to prioritize alerts based on severity and potential impact.

This ensures that SOC staff focus on the most critical issues, optimizing their time and resources.

- **Scalable Cloud-Based Solutions**: Implement cloud-based SOC solutions that offer scalability to suit your business needs. Cloud-based tools can be more cost-effective, reducing the need for on-premises hardware and maintenance.

- **Regularly Review SOC Processes**: Conduct periodic reviews of SOC processes and technologies to identify areas for improvement and cost savings.

- **Efficient Staff Training and Development**: Invest in comprehensive training to develop a highly skilled SOC team capable of handling diverse threats efficiently. A well-trained team can work more effectively, reducing the need for a larger staff.

- **Utilize Advanced Analytics and AI**: Implement advanced analytics and AI to assist in threat detection and response. These technologies can enhance the effectiveness of the SOC team, allowing them to manage more threats with fewer resources.

- **Performance Metrics and KPIs**: Establish clear performance metrics and KPIs to continually assess the SOC's effectiveness and efficiency, ensuring resources are used optimally.

- **Shared Intelligence and Collaboration**: Engage in information sharing and collaboration with other organizations and security communities. This can provide access to a broader range of threat intelligence, improving effectiveness without significant cost increases.

- **Optimize Shift Scheduling**: Efficiently manage shift scheduling to ensure that the SOC is adequately staffed during peak times while avoiding overstaffing during quieter periods.

By implementing these strategies, businesses can operate a highly effective SOC that provides comprehensive security monitoring and response capabilities, while also being mindful of budgetary constraints.

Case Study on Implementing Cost-Effective Robust Cloud Network Security Strategies

In my experience working closely with a rapidly expanding e-commerce company, I've witnessed firsthand the challenges of ensuring robust cloud network security while keeping costs in check. As the company's customer base grew and its reliance on cloud services increased, there was a pressing need to bolster its security measures to safeguard sensitive customer data, and intellectual property, and maintain regulatory compliance.

Here's what I observed:

Growing Cloud Footprint: The company experienced rapid growth in its cloud infrastructure, utilizing services from multiple providers to meet business demands. Managing security across this diverse and expanding landscape posed a significant challenge.

Cost Constraints: With budget limitations as a mid-sized company, it was essential to implement effective security measures without significantly increasing operational costs.

Compliance Requirements: Given the nature of the e-commerce industry, strict adherence to regulatory standards such as PCI DSS for payment data protection and GDPR for customer data privacy was imperative.

Strategies Implemented:

- **Cloud Security Assessment**: A thorough assessment of the existing cloud infrastructure was conducted to identify vulnerabilities, misconfigurations, and potential security gaps. Cloud-native security tools and third-party solutions were utilized to enhance visibility into network traffic and monitor security events.

- **Zero Trust Network Architecture**: Adopting a Zero Trust model ensured that no user or system was trusted by default, implementing micro-segmentation to isolate workloads, applications, and data.

- **Identity and Access Management (IAM)**: Strengthening IAM policies enforced the principle of least privilege, with the implementation of Multi-Factor Authentication (MFA) enhancing user access security.

- **Encryption and Data Protection**: Encryption for data in transit and at rest was enabled, while data loss prevention (DLP) measures were implemented to monitor and control the transfer of sensitive information.

- **Automated Security Controls**: Automation was leveraged for security controls, allowing real-time response to security incidents and automated enforcement of policies.

Regular Security Training and Awareness: Regular security training sessions were conducted for employees to promote awareness about cloud security best practices, fostering a culture of security consciousness.

Results and Benefits:

- **Improved Security Posture**: The implementation of robust cloud network security measures significantly enhanced the company's security posture, reducing the risk of data breaches and unauthorized access.

- **Cost Savings through Automation**: Automation of security controls and incident response processes led to operational efficiency, reducing manual effort and optimizing cloud resource utilization.

- **Compliance Adherence**: The implemented measures ensured compliance with industry-specific regulations, providing assurance to customers and stakeholders about data security.

- **Minimal Disruption to Operations**: Phased implementation of security measures minimized disruptions to ongoing business operations, allowing the company to maintain focus on customer service and growth.

- **Enhanced Customer Trust**: Visible commitment to robust security measures enhanced customer trust, fostering increased loyalty and confidence in the company's ability to protect sensitive information.

Conclusion: Through strategic implementation of cost-effective cloud network security measures, the company successfully addressed the challenges of securing a growing and diverse cloud environment. Balancing security and cost-effectiveness contributed to its continued success in the competitive e-commerce landscape.

Summary:

Implementing Cost Effective Robust Cloud Network Security Measures in Cloud

- *Employ cost-effective antivirus software and Extended Detection and Response (XDR) solutions.*

- *Utilize monitoring, reviewing, and auditing processes to ensure cost-effectiveness.*

- *Manage Cloud Security Posture Management to identify misconfigurations and compliance violations.*

- *Implement access and privileged management protocols to mitigate internal threats.*

- *Deploy AI-powered Zero-day threat protection tools to bolster detection and response capabilities.*

- *Establish a Security Operations Center to adhere to regulatory requirements.*

Exercise:

Objective: To devise a strategy for implementing cost-effective and robust cloud network security measures that enhance security posture without significantly increasing operational costs.

Steps:

Current State Assessment:

- Evaluate your organization's current cloud network security posture, including existing tools, processes, and vulnerabilities.

- Identify potential security gaps, compliance requirements, and areas for improvement based on industry standards and best practices.

Define Security Objectives:

- Clarify the specific security objectives and priorities of your organization, considering factors such as data protection, regulatory compliance, and threat mitigation.

- Determine the level of security required for different types of data, applications, and workloads hosted in the cloud.

Cost Analysis and Budget Allocation:

- Conduct a cost analysis to understand the financial implications of implementing cloud network security measures.

- Allocate budgetary resources based on the identified security priorities, balancing the need for security with cost-effectiveness.

Zero Trust Network Architecture:

- Explore the adoption of a Zero Trust network architecture to enhance security posture and minimize the risk of lateral movement by potential attackers.

- Evaluate the feasibility of implementing micro-segmentation to isolate workloads and applications within the cloud environment.

Identity and Access Management (IAM):

- Strengthen IAM policies and procedures to enforce the principle of least privilege and ensure granular control over user access and permissions.

- Consider implementing Multi-Factor Authentication (MFA) to add an additional layer of security for user authentication.

Encryption and Data Protection:

- Implement encryption for data both in transit and at rest using cloud-native encryption features and protocols.

- Evaluate the implementation of data loss prevention (DLP) measures to monitor and control the movement of sensitive data within the cloud environment.

Automated Security Controls:

- Explore the use of automation for security controls, incident response, and threat detection to improve operational efficiency and reduce manual effort.

- Identify opportunities to leverage cloud-native security tools and third-party solutions for automated threat detection and remediation.

Employee Training and Awareness:

- Develop a comprehensive security training program for employees to raise awareness about cloud network security best practices.

- Encourage a culture of security consciousness and accountability throughout the organization, empowering employees to identify and report potential security threats.

Pilot Testing and Implementation:

- Conduct pilot testing of selected security measures to assess their effectiveness and impact on the cloud environment.

- Implement security measures in a phased approach, starting with critical assets and gradually expanding coverage to other areas of the cloud infrastructure.

Monitoring and Continuous Improvement:

- Implement robust monitoring and logging mechanisms to track security events, detect anomalies, and investigate potential security incidents.

- Establish a process for continuous improvement, regularly reviewing and updating security policies, procedures, and controls based on emerging threats and evolving business requirements.

Conclusion: By following these steps, organizations can develop a comprehensive plan for implementing cost-effective and robust cloud network security measures that enhance security posture while optimizing operational costs. The exercise helps align security objectives with business priorities, ensuring that security investments contribute to the overall success and resilience of the organization in the cloud environment.

Chapter 4

Business Transformation through the Implementation of Generative AI

Have you ever considered how the decisions you make today about cloud security and cost management will shape the future of your business? Business transformation through the implementation of Generative AI offers a roadmap to navigate the complexities of the digital age and future-proof your business.

Generative AI is a subset of artificial intelligence, that focuses on creating new content, data, or solutions by learning from existing data sets. Unlike traditional AI models that are primarily geared towards analysis and decision-making, generative AI is about producing novel outputs. Here's a closer look:

What It Does: Generative AI can create text, images, videos, and more. It's capable of tasks like writing code, composing music, generating realistic human faces, or even drafting email responses.

How It Works: It typically uses advanced machine learning algorithms like Generative Adversarial Networks (GANs) or Variational Autoencoders (VAEs). These models train on a large dataset and learn to generate outputs that are similar but not identical.

Business Applications: In business, generative AI can be used for a variety of purposes. This includes creating personalized marketing content, generating realistic product prototypes, automating the design process, or even developing unique solutions to complex problems.

Enhancing Creativity and Efficiency: Generative AI can augment human creativity by providing new ideas and perspectives. It also enhances efficiency by automating certain creative tasks.

Customization and Personalization: Businesses can use generative AI to offer highly customized and personalized products or services, catering to individual customer preferences at scale.

Challenges and Considerations: While promising, generative AI also poses challenges like ensuring data privacy, avoiding biases in generated content, and maintaining authenticity and originality.

Future Potential: As technology evolves, generative AI is expected to play a significant role in shaping various industries, from entertainment and marketing to product development and beyond.

AI-Driven Threat Detection and Mitigation in Business Network Environments Expansion

AI-driven threat detection and mitigation in business network environments play a crucial role in safeguarding digital assets and maintaining operational integrity. Here's an expanded view of how AI is transforming threat detection and mitigation:

- **Advanced Threat Detection**: AI algorithms can analyse network traffic in real time to identify patterns indicative of cyber threats. This includes detecting malware, ransomware, phishing attempts, and other sophisticated attacks that traditional methods might miss.

- **Predictive Threat Intelligence**: AI goes beyond reactive measures by predicting potential security threats before they materialize. It analyses historical data and current trends to anticipate and prepare for future attacks.

- **Automated Incident Response**: Upon detecting a threat, AI-driven systems can automatically initiate responses such as isolating affected systems, blocking malicious IP addresses, or deploying patches, significantly reducing response time and containing damage.

- **Behavioural Analysis**: AI tools are adapted to behavioural analysis, identifying deviations from normal network behaviour that may indicate a security breach, insider threat, or compromised account.

- **Continuous Learning and Adaptation**: AI models continuously learn from new data, improving their accuracy and effectiveness over time. This is crucial in the ever-evolving landscape of cyber threats.

- **Enhanced Data Security**: AI can encrypt, monitor, and manage data access more efficiently, ensuring sensitive information is protected against unauthorized access or leaks.

- **Scalable Security Solutions**: AI-driven security solutions can scale with the growth of the business network, providing consistent protection regardless of the size or complexity of the network.

- **Integration with Existing Systems**: AI can be integrated with existing security infrastructures, enhancing their capabilities without the need for complete overhauls.

- **Customized Security Policies**: AI enables customization of security policies based on specific business needs and risk profiles, ensuring a more targeted and effective security approach.

- **User and Entity Behavior Analytics (UEBA)**: AI-driven UEBA tools analyze user behaviour and detect anomalies that may indicate a threat, such as unusual login locations or times, and access patterns.

- **Reduced False Positives**: AI's advanced analysis capabilities lead to a reduction in false positives, allowing security teams to focus on genuine threats and avoid wasting resources.

- **Compliance and Reporting**: AI assists in maintaining compliance with various data protection and privacy regulations by automating compliance monitoring and generating detailed reports for audits.

AI-driven threat detection and mitigation are redefining business network security, offering more proactive, intelligent, and responsive approaches to protecting against cyber threats in the digital age.

Security Automation through Generative AI for Business Resilience and Continuity

Security automation through Generative AI is a significant advancement in enhancing business resilience and continuity. This approach involves leveraging AI's ability to generate responses and solutions autonomously, thereby streamlining security processes and fortifying defences. Here's a detailed look at its implications:

- **Proactive Threat Detection**: Generative AI can simulate various attack scenarios, helping businesses anticipate and prepare for potential threats. By generating models of cyber-attack strategies, it allows organizations to strengthen their defences proactively.

- **Automated Response and Remediation**: In the event of a security breach, generative AI can automatically generate response strategies to isolate and mitigate the threat. This rapid response limits damage and helps maintain business operations.

- **Dynamic Risk Assessment**: Generative AI continuously evaluates the security landscape, generating up-to-date risk assessments. This dynamic approach ensures that security measures evolve in line with emerging threats, maintaining a robust defence.

- **Customized Security Solutions**: By analysing a business's specific security needs, generative AI can create tailored security protocols and configurations, ensuring a close fit to the unique requirements of each organization.

- **Enhanced Incident Analysis**: Post-incident, generative AI can analyse the breach's nature and origins. It then generates reports and recommendations for strengthening security measures, turning every incident into a learning opportunity.

- **Streamlining Compliance**: Generative AI aids in maintaining compliance with evolving regulations by automatically generating the necessary documentation and ensuring that security systems meet the latest standards.

- **Disaster Recovery Planning**: AI can simulate various disaster scenarios and generate effective recovery plans. These AI-created plans help businesses prepare for and quickly recover from disruptive events, ensuring minimal downtime.

- **Employee Training and Simulation**: Generative AI can develop training programs and simulations for employees, enhancing their understanding of security protocols and preparing them for potential cyber threats.

- **Optimization of Security Resources**: By automating routine security tasks, generative AI allows human security professionals to focus on more complex and strategic activities, optimizing the use of security resources.

- **Future-Proofing Security Strategies**: Generative AI's ability to predict future threats and generate appropriate defence mechanisms helps businesses stay ahead of the curve, future-proofing their security strategies.

In summary, security automation through Generative AI represents a significant leap in building resilient and continuous business operations. It not only enhances existing security measures but also introduces new capabilities, making businesses more agile, prepared, and secure in an ever-changing digital environment.

Case Study: Security Automation through Generative AI for Business Resilience and Continuity

In my experience collaborating with a multinational financial services company, I've witnessed the imperative need to bolster cybersecurity capabilities to mitigate evolving cyber threats and ensure business resilience and continuity. With vast amounts of sensitive financial data and regulatory compliance requirements, the company embarked on a journey to explore innovative solutions to automate security operations and fortify its defences against cyber-attacks.

Here's what I observed:

Cybersecurity Threat Landscape: The company confronted an increasingly sophisticated and dynamic cyber threat landscape, including ransomware attacks, phishing attempts, and insider threats.

Manual Security Operations: Heavy reliance on manual processes for security operations, incident response, and threat detection led to delays in identifying and mitigating security incidents.

Resource Constraints: Limited resources, including skilled cybersecurity personnel and budgetary constraints, posed significant challenges in effectively managing and responding to security threats.

Strategies Implemented:

Generative AI for Threat Detection: Leveraged generative AI algorithms to analyze large volumes of security data, identify patterns, and detect anomalies indicative of potential security threats. The organization deployed AI-driven threat detection solutions like Azure Sentinel, and Microsoft Defender for Endpoint, capable of identifying emerging threats and sophisticated attack techniques in real-time.

Automated Incident Response: Integrated generative AI capabilities into the organization's incident response processes to automate the detection, analysis, and remediation of security incidents. Implementation of AI-driven playbooks and response workflows in Azure, streamlined decision-making and accelerated response times.

Predictive Analytics and Risk Assessment: Utilization of generative AI models like Prisma Cloud CSPM tool, to perform predictive analytics and risk assessments, and identify potential security vulnerabilities before they could be exploited by adversaries. Application of AI-driven risk-scoring mechanisms prioritized security events and focused resources on the most critical threats and vulnerabilities.

Continuous Learning and Adaptation: Implementation of a feedback loop mechanism to continuously train and refine generative AI models based on new threat intelligence and historical data. The promotion of collaboration and knowledge sharing between human analysts and AI systems enhanced the effectiveness and accuracy of threat detection and response.

Results and Benefits:

Improved Threat Detection and Response: The implementation of generative AI-driven security automation solutions enhanced the company's threat detection capabilities and response to security incidents. Faster response times, reduced mean time to detect (MTTD) and mean time to respond (MTTR) metrics and minimized the impact of security breaches were achieved.

Enhanced Business Resilience and Continuity: By automating security operations and incident response, the company strengthened its business resilience and continuity, minimizing disruption to critical business processes and services. The organization demonstrated its ability to adapt and respond to evolving cyber threats, ensuring uninterrupted operations and maintaining customer trust.

Cost Savings and Operational Efficiency: Adoption of generative AI-driven security automation solutions resulted in cost savings and operational efficiencies by reducing manual effort, improving resource allocation, and optimizing security operations. A higher return on investment (ROI) of 100% from cybersecurity investments was achieved, leveraging AI-driven technologies to maximize the value of the security infrastructure.

Proactive Risk Management: Through predictive analytics and risk assessments powered by generative AI, the company gained deeper insights into potential security risks and vulnerabilities, enabling proactive risk management and mitigation strategies. Prioritization of security initiatives and resource allocation based on AI-driven risk scoring mechanisms focused on addressing the most significant threats to its infrastructure and data assets.

Conclusion: By embracing security automation through generative AI, the company transformed its cybersecurity operations, achieving greater resilience, continuity, and efficiency in the face of evolving cyber threats. The organization demonstrated the power of AI-driven technologies in enhancing threat detection, incident response, and risk management, positioning itself as a leader in cybersecurity innovation and best practices.

Real-world examples of AI-driven Cloud Security tools

Microsoft Azure's Azure Sentinel

A real-world example of AI cloud security tools in action is Microsoft Azure's Azure Sentinel. Azure Sentinel is a cloud-native security information and event management (SIEM) service that uses AI and machine learning to analyse vast amounts of data across an organization's cloud and on-premises environments. It helps detect and respond to threats in real time by correlating data from various sources, including logs, alerts, and security events.

Azure Sentinel employs AI algorithms to identify suspicious activities, anomalous behaviours, and potential security threats across the entire infrastructure. It can automatically prioritize alerts, investigate incidents, and even orchestrate responses, saving valuable time for security analysts. By leveraging AI, Azure Sentinel enhances threat detection accuracy and reduces false positives, allowing organizations to focus their resources on addressing genuine security issues efficiently.

Moreover, Azure Sentinel's scalability and cloud-based architecture make it a cost-effective solution for organizations of all sizes. It eliminates the need for costly infrastructure investments and allows businesses to pay only for the resources they consume. This flexibility and affordability make Azure Sentinel a compelling example of how AI-powered cloud security tools can enhance cybersecurity while remaining cost-effective in real-world scenarios.

Palo Alto Firewall

Palo Alto Networks offers AI-based cloud network security tools, including its firewall solutions, designed to provide advanced threat detection, prevention, and response capabilities. Here are some ways Palo Alto's firewall offerings incorporate AI and cloud-based security features:

Threat Prevention with AI/ML: Palo Alto's firewall solutions leverage artificial intelligence (AI) and machine learning (ML) algorithms to analyze network traffic patterns, detect anomalies, and identify potential threats in real-time. By continuously learning from new data and evolving threats, these AI-driven capabilities enhance the firewall's ability to detect and prevent sophisticated cyber-attacks.

Behavioural Analytics: Palo Alto's firewalls utilize behavioural analytics to monitor user and device behaviour across the network. By establishing baseline behaviour profiles for users, applications, and devices, the firewall can identify deviations from normal patterns that may indicate malicious activity or unauthorized access attempts.

Automated Threat Response: Palo Alto's firewall solutions feature automated threat response capabilities that can automatically block or quarantine malicious traffic, isolate compromised devices, and apply security policies to mitigate security risks in real-time. This helps organizations respond swiftly to security incidents and reduce the impact of cyber threats.

Cloud Integration and Management: Palo Alto's firewall solutions can be integrated with cloud-based security platforms and management consoles, enabling centralized visibility and control across hybrid and multi-cloud environments. This allows organizations to extend consistent security policies and enforcement mechanisms to their cloud infrastructure and applications.

Threat Intelligence and Feed Integration: Palo Alto's firewalls integrate with threat intelligence feeds and cloud-based threat intelligence platforms to provide up-to-date information on emerging threats, vulnerabilities, and attack trends. By leveraging threat intelligence, organizations can enhance their threat detection capabilities and proactively defend against evolving cyber threats.

Scalability and Performance: Palo Alto's firewall solutions are designed to scale seamlessly to meet the growing demands of modern cloud-based environments. By leveraging cloud-native architectures and technologies, these solutions deliver high-performance security capabilities while ensuring scalability and flexibility to accommodate dynamic workloads and traffic patterns.

Overall, Palo Alto's firewall solutions serve as AI-based cloud network security tools that help organizations protect their digital assets and infrastructure from a wide range of cyber threats, while also providing visibility, control, and compliance across their cloud environments.

Summary:

The Security Automation through Generative AI for Business Resilience and Continuity:

- Leveraging AI for threat detection and mitigation can facilitate business transformation and expansion.

- Employing security automation via Generative AI enhances business resilience and continuity.

- Implementing Generative AI tools such as Microsoft Azure Sentinel and Palo Alto Firewall enables security automation.

Exercise:

Objective: To develop a plan for implementing security automation through generative AI to improve business resilience and continuity.

Steps:

Assessment of Current Security Operations:

- Evaluate your organization's current security operations, including threat detection, incident response, and risk management processes.

- Identify any inefficiencies, gaps, or bottlenecks in the existing security operations that could benefit from automation.

Understanding Generative AI for Security:

- Educate key stakeholders on the concept of generative AI and its application in cybersecurity.

- Explore case studies and examples of how generative AI is used for threat detection, anomaly detection, and predictive analytics in security operations.

Identify Use Cases for Automation:

- Identify specific use cases within your organization's security operations that could benefit from automation through generative AI.

- Examples include automated threat detection, incident response orchestration, predictive risk assessment, and security analytics.

Define Security Automation Objectives:

- Define clear objectives for implementing security automation through generative AI, aligned with business resilience and continuity goals.

- Determine key performance indicators (KPIs) and metrics for measuring the effectiveness and impact of security automation initiatives.

Select Suitable Generative AI Tools and Technologies:

- Research and evaluate generative AI tools and technologies available in the market for security automation.

- Consider factors such as accuracy, scalability, interoperability, ease of integration, and vendor support in your selection process.

Develop Implementation Plan:

- Develop a phased implementation plan for deploying security automation solutions powered by generative AI.

- Define the scope, timeline, and resource requirements for each phase of the implementation, considering factors such as organizational readiness and technical complexity.

Integration with Existing Security Infrastructure:

- Ensure seamless integration of generative AI-driven security automation solutions with existing security infrastructure, tools, and processes.

- Establish data pipelines and integration points for ingesting security data from diverse sources and feeding insights back into operational workflows.

Training and Change Management:

- Provide comprehensive training and education to security personnel and other stakeholders involved in the implementation and operation of generative AI-driven security automation solutions.

- Foster a culture of continuous learning and adaptation to ensure the successful adoption and utilization of automation technologies.

Continuous Monitoring and Improvement:

- Establish mechanisms for continuous monitoring, evaluation, and improvement of generative AI-driven security automation initiatives.

- Implement feedback loops and analytics dashboards to track KPIs, identify performance trends, and drive continuous optimization and refinement of automation processes.

Testing and Validation:

- Conduct thorough testing and validation of generative AI-driven security automation solutions in a controlled environment before full-scale deployment.

- Perform simulated cyber-attack scenarios and incident response drills to assess the effectiveness and readiness of automated security controls and workflows.

Conclusion: By following these steps, organizations can develop a structured approach for implementing security automation through generative AI to enhance business resilience and continuity in the face of cyber threats. The exercise helps organizations leverage the power of AI-driven technologies to automate repetitive tasks, improve response times, and adapt to evolving threat landscapes, ultimately strengthening their overall security posture and readiness.

Chapter 5

Governance for Business Advancement

By navigating these realms with strategic foresight and ethical consideration, businesses can not only enhance their operational effectiveness and financial health but also lead the way in shaping a more sustainable, equitable, and technologically advanced future.

Governance Frameworks for Secure, Efficient, Ethical, and Innovative Business Network Operations in Cloud

Establishing governance frameworks for secure, efficient, ethical, and innovative business network operations is essential in today's digital business landscape. Such frameworks ensure that network operations are conducted responsibly, align with business objectives, and adhere to ethical standards while fostering innovation and efficiency. Here's how to build and implement these frameworks:

Security Governance

- **Risk Management Framework:** Develop a comprehensive risk management framework to identify, assess, mitigate, and monitor network security risks.

- **Data Security Policies**: Implement policies for data protection, including encryption, access controls, and breach response protocols.

- **Cybersecurity Standards Compliance**: Ensure compliance with international cybersecurity standards like ISO 27001, NIST frameworks, and industry-specific regulations.

- **Incident Response Plan**: Create a robust incident response plan for quick and effective action in case of security breaches.

Efficiency and Performance Governance

- **Network Performance Monitoring**: Deploy tools for continuous monitoring of network performance, identifying areas for optimization.

- **Resource Management**: Implement strategies for efficient allocation and use of network resources, including bandwidth, storage, and computing power.

- **Technology Upgrades and Maintenance**: Regularly update network infrastructure and software to ensure optimal performance and efficiency.

- **Best Practices and Benchmarking**: Adopt industry best practices and benchmark against peer organizations for continuous improvement.

Ethical Governance

- **AI Ethics Policies**: As mentioned earlier, integrate AI ethics policies focusing on transparency, fairness, privacy, and accountability.

- **Data Privacy Compliance**: Adhere to data privacy laws like GDPR, HIPAA, and others, ensuring ethical handling of personal and sensitive data.

- **Employee Conduct and Training**: Establish a code of conduct for network operations staff and provide regular training on ethical practices.

- **Stakeholder Engagement**: Engage with stakeholders, including customers and suppliers, to ensure that network operations align with ethical expectations.

Innovation Governance

- **Innovation Management Process**: Create processes to identify, evaluate, and implement innovative technologies and practices in network operations.

- **Research and Development Investment**: Allocate budget and resources for R&D to explore new technologies and methodologies.

- **Cross-Functional Innovation Teams**: Form cross-functional teams to foster diverse thinking and collaborative innovation in network operations.

- **Partnerships with Tech Companies and Academia**: Collaborate with technology companies, startups, and academic institutions for fresh insights and innovative solutions.

Compliance and Legal Governance

- **Regulatory Compliance Monitoring**: Regularly monitor and ensure compliance with all relevant legal and regulatory requirements.

- **Legal Review of Contracts and Agreements**: Have network-related contracts and agreements reviewed by legal experts to ensure compliance and protect the company's interests.

- **Licensing and Intellectual Property Management**: Manage software licenses, patents, and intellectual property rights related to network operations.

Continuous Improvement and Adaptation

- **Feedback Mechanisms**: Implement feedback mechanisms from users and stakeholders to continuously improve network operations.

- **Adaptability to Change**: Build agility into the network governance framework to adapt to technological advancements and market changes.

- **Regular Audits and Assessments**: Conduct regular audits and assessments of network operations to identify areas for improvement.

Governance Structure and Leadership

- **Dedicated Governance Body**: Establish a dedicated governance body or committee to oversee and coordinate all aspects of network governance.

- **Clear Leadership and Accountability**: Assign clear leadership roles and accountability for various aspects of network governance.

- **Stakeholder Representation**: Ensure representation of all relevant stakeholders, including IT, business units, legal, and compliance, in the governance body.

Budget Governance

- **Strategic Allocation**: Investing in AI and network advancements should align with long-term business goals and ROI expectations.

- **Cost Management**: Balancing the costs of adopting cutting-edge technologies while maintaining operational and financial stability.

- **Performance Monitoring**: Regularly assessing the financial performance of technology investments against set benchmarks.

Documentation and Policy Management

- **Comprehensive Documentation**: Maintain thorough documentation of governance policies, procedures, and frameworks.

- **Accessible Policy Repository**: Make governance documentation easily accessible to all relevant personnel and stakeholders.

In conclusion, setting different Governance frameworks is the cornerstone of a modern, responsible, and innovative business. The journey is complex and multifaceted, but the rewards are significant – for the business, its stakeholders, and society at large.

Case Study: Governance Frameworks for Secure, Efficient, Ethical, and Innovative Business Network Operations in the Cloud

In my professional experience working with a multinational conglomerate, I've observed the challenges and solutions surrounding governance frameworks for secure, efficient, ethical, and innovative business network operations in the cloud.

Here's what I've seen:

- **Security Concerns**: With sensitive business data and intellectual property stored in the cloud, the company faced heightened security concerns, including data breaches, insider threats, and compliance risks.

- **Operational Efficiency**: The decentralized nature of cloud operations across subsidiaries led to inefficiencies in resource management, procurement, and service delivery.

- **Ethical Considerations**: Prioritizing ethical considerations such as data privacy, transparency, and accountability was crucial for upholding the company's reputation and stakeholder trust.

- **Innovation Imperative**: To stay competitive, the company sought to foster a culture of innovation and agility while maintaining security and compliance requirements.

Strategies Implemented:

- **Establishment of Governance Frameworks**: Tailored governance frameworks were developed for each business unit, aligning with industry standards and best practices. These frameworks encompassed policies, procedures, controls, and metrics to effectively govern cloud adoption, usage, and operations.

- **Security-First Approach**: A security-first approach to cloud governance was adopted, prioritizing data protection, encryption, access controls, and threat detection mechanisms. Identity and access management (IAM) policies, encryption protocols, and network segmentation strategies were implemented to mitigate security risks.

- **Operational Excellence**: The focus was on optimizing cloud operations for efficiency, cost-effectiveness, and performance. Cloud management platforms, automation tools, and DevOps practices were leveraged to streamline the provisioning, monitoring, and management of cloud resources.

- **Ethical Guidelines and Compliance**: Ethical guidelines and compliance frameworks were established to govern data privacy, consent management, and responsible AI usage in the cloud. Regular audits, assessments, and compliance checks ensured adherence to regulatory requirements and industry standards.

- **Innovation Enablement**: A culture of innovation was fostered by providing resources, training, and support for experimentation and exploration of emerging technologies in the cloud. Cross-functional collaboration, knowledge sharing, and experimentation with cloud-native services and solutions were encouraged.

Results and Benefits:

- **Enhanced Security Posture**: Robust governance frameworks strengthened the company's security posture, reducing the risk of data breaches and cyber threats in the cloud environment.

- **Improved Operational Efficiency**: Streamlined cloud operations and automation initiatives resulted in improved efficiency, resource optimization, and cost savings across business units.

- **Ethical Leadership**: Demonstrating ethical leadership by prioritizing data privacy, transparency, and accountability earned the trust and confidence of customers, partners, and regulators.

- **Fostered Innovation**: Governance frameworks provided a foundation for innovation, enabling business units to experiment with new technologies, services, and business models securely and compliantly.

- **Business Agility**: Greater business agility and resilience allowed the company to adapt to changing market dynamics, customer demands, and regulatory requirements more effectively.

Conclusion: By implementing governance frameworks for secure, efficient, ethical, and innovative business network operations in the cloud, the company showcased its commitment to excellence, integrity, and sustainability in the digital age. A proactive approach to cloud governance enabled the mitigation of risks, drove operational excellence, and unlocked new opportunities for growth and differentiation in a rapidly evolving business landscape.

Summary:

Governance Frameworks for Secure Business Network Operations in Cloud

- *Security Governance is instituted to guarantee that network operations align with business objectives.*

- *Governance should be implemented across various levels, including budget, performance, innovation, and legal domains.*

Exercise:

Objective: To design a comprehensive governance framework for secure, efficient, ethical, and innovative business network operations in the cloud.

Instructions:

- Begin by identifying key components of a governance framework that align with the principles of security, efficiency, ethics, and innovation in cloud network operations.

- Evaluate existing governance frameworks and best practices in the industry, considering frameworks such as COBIT, NIST, ISO 27001, and CSA Cloud Controls Matrix.

- Outline the specific requirements and considerations for each aspect of the governance framework, including:

  - **Security:** Identify protocols, encryption standards, access controls, and incident response procedures.

  - **Efficiency:** Streamline processes, automate tasks, optimize resource utilization, and monitor performance metrics.

  - **Ethics:** Establish guidelines for data privacy, compliance with regulations (such as GDPR, and CCPA), and ethical use of AI and machine learning algorithms.

- o **Innovation:** Encourage experimentation, foster a culture of continuous improvement, and promote the adoption of emerging technologies while managing associated risks.

- Develop policies, procedures, and guidelines for implementing and enforcing the governance framework within your organization's cloud network operations.

- Consider the role of stakeholders, including executives, IT teams, security specialists, compliance officers, and end-users, in adhering to and upholding the governance framework.

- Incorporate mechanisms for regular review, assessment, and refinement of the governance framework to adapt to evolving threats, technologies, and business needs.

- Collaborate with relevant departments and teams to ensure buy-in and alignment with the governance framework's objectives and principles.

- Conduct training and awareness programs to educate employees on their roles and responsibilities in maintaining secure, efficient, ethical, and innovative cloud network operations.

- Finally, evaluate the effectiveness of the governance framework through periodic audits, assessments, and feedback mechanisms, and iterate as necessary to address any gaps or areas for improvement.

Deliverables:

- A detailed outline of the governance framework, including components, requirements, and considerations.

- Policies, procedures, and guidelines document for implementing and enforcing the governance framework.

- Training materials and awareness programs for educating employees on their roles and responsibilities.

- Mechanisms for ongoing review, assessment, and refinement of the governance framework.

Reflection: Reflect on the challenges encountered and lessons learned during the development of the governance framework. Consider how the framework aligns with your organization's strategic objectives and contributes to enhancing cloud network operations in terms of security, efficiency, ethics, and innovation.

Chapter -6

Exploring Business Success Stories achieved through the Implementation of Cloud Network Security, Efficient Cost Management, and the Integration of Generative AI.

The future of business is being written in the cloud, but not all stories have a happy ending. Some of the scripts to ensure your business's story thrives in the digital age, blending advanced technology with savvy business strategy to turn potential risks into success stories.

The Financial Institution enhances governance by mitigating cloud security breaches.

In my experience working with a financial institution, I've witnessed the challenges and solutions surrounding the improvement of governance by reducing cloud security breaches.

Challenges: The client aimed to establish a solid cloud security foundation with a well-architected framework that met regulatory and compliance requirements while ensuring effective cloud security posture management.

Solution:

- Conducted comprehensive cloud security posture assessments using a combination of manual analysis and automated assessment tools.

- Developed a detailed architecture roadmap aligned with the client's regulatory needs and industry standards to address security concerns effectively.

- Recommended technical guidelines focusing on network misconfigurations, vulnerabilities based on best practices, and other identified issues to bolster the security posture.

Outcome:

Increased visibility and governance were achieved through the reduction of the impact of cloud security breaches. The implemented measures enhanced the overall security posture of the client's cloud environment, leading to better adherence to regulatory requirements and improved management of cloud security risks.

The technology firm enhances its management of cloud security posture in a cost-effective manner.

In my experience working with a technology firm, I've seen how they addressed the challenge of improving cost-effective cloud security posture management.

Challenge: The tech firm encountered escalating cybersecurity threats and escalating operational expenses associated with their on-premises infrastructure.

Solution:

- Deployed robust cloud network security measures, including next-gen firewalls, NSG/ASG rules, and optimized routing policies.

- Employed cost-effective cloud security posture management tools for continuous monitoring and proactive prevention oversight.

- Integrated generative AI for advanced threat detection, leveraging its capability to identify zero-day threats effectively.

Outcome:

- Significantly enhanced the overall security posture, reducing the likelihood of successful cyberattacks.

- Achieved cost savings through the optimization of cloud resources and the implementation of efficient security measures.

- Established the company as an industry leader with a strong commitment to cybersecurity.

The manufacturing company improved operational efficiencies and decreased operational expenditure (OPEX).

In my experience with a manufacturing company, I witnessed the achievement of increased operational efficiencies and a reduction in OPEX costs.

Challenge: The company faced challenges such as low security across multiple geographic locations due to the absence of security best practices. It also grappled with high-risk multi-vendor inconsistent security product development and lacked monitoring and incident management controls in the hybrid cloud environment.

Solution:

- Established a framework for existing and onboarding new security services.

- Implemented multiple security controls in Azure and AWS using standardized templates and accelerators, thereby enhancing overall security.

Outcome:

- Optimized team structure and governance model, leading to better coordination and response.

- Ensured business continuity plan across the company's managed services operation.

- Implemented proactive tracking and improvement in the information security posture.

The healthcare company enhances compliance by securing sensitive health data.

In my experience with a healthcare company, I've observed the strides they made in improving compliance by securing sensitive health data.

Challenge: The healthcare company grappled with challenges concerning the security of sensitive health data stored in the cloud. They also faced hurdles in ensuring compliance with healthcare regulations and managing the associated costs of healthcare data storage.

Solution:

- Implemented stringent cloud network security measures, encompassing access controls, encryption protocols, and regular monitoring to safeguard sensitive health data.

- Leveraged generative AI technology for anomaly detection in healthcare data, thereby enhancing the organization's ability to detect potential threats effectively.

- Adopted cost-effective cloud storage solutions and optimized data management processes to address the financial aspect of data storage.

Outcome:

- Achieved robust security measures for sensitive health data, ensuring compliance with stringent healthcare regulations.

- Significantly reduced storage costs by implementing efficient data management practices and leveraging cost-effective cloud solutions.

- Gained a competitive edge by demonstrating a strong commitment to both security and cost efficiency, enhancing the company's reputation in the healthcare sector.

The Technology Corporation enhances both cost efficiency and security through the utilization of AI-enhanced security measures.

In my experience with a leading Technology Corporation, I've witnessed their journey to enhance cost-effectiveness and security by leveraging AI-enhanced security solutions.

Challenges: The Technology Corporation faced significant challenges in ensuring robust security measures, managing costs effectively, and adopting advanced technologies for threat detection and response.

Solution:

Cloud Network Security Implementation:

- Deployed Next-Generation Firewalls, NSG/ASG rules, and routing policies to establish a secure network infrastructure.

- Implemented advanced access management and privileged management solutions to regulate access to critical resources.

- Integrated monitoring, reviewing, and auditing processes to maintain continuous visibility and compliance with security policies.

Efficient Cost Management:

- Optimized cloud security spending by transitioning to a pay-as-you-go model for security services.

- Implemented automated cost management tools for real-time monitoring and control of expenditures.

- Conducted regular cost reviews and audits to identify areas for optimization and efficiency improvements.

Integration of Generative AI:

- Implemented generative AI algorithms for advanced threat detection and response, leveraging sophisticated machine learning techniques.

- Deployed AI-powered antivirus and XDR solutions to identify and mitigate emerging threats in real time.

- Utilized generative AI for anomaly detection and behaviour analysis, enhancing proactive security measures.

Outcome:

Enhanced Security:

The company experienced a significant improvement in security posture, witnessing reduced vulnerabilities and enhanced threat detection capabilities.

Cost Efficiency:

The implementation of cost management practices led to optimized spending, reduced wastage, and improved resource utilization.

Advanced Threat Detection:

The integration of generative AI facilitated early detection and mitigation of zero-day threats and advanced persistent threats (APTs).

Business Success:

With a secure and cost-efficient cloud environment, the Company achieved greater operational resilience, gained customer trust, and secured a competitive advantage in the market.

Financial enterprises improved data analytics by finding a balance among cost, security, and Generative AI.

In my experience with a financial services firm, I've observed how they improved data analytics while balancing cost, security, and Generative AI.

Challenges: The financial enterprise encountered escalating cybersecurity threats, increasing operational costs, and the imperative to enhance data analytics capabilities to maintain competitiveness.

Solution:

Cloud Network Security:

Migrated infrastructure to a secure cloud environment, implementing next-generation firewalls, network security groups, and access controls to safeguard sensitive financial data.

Efficient Cost Management:

Implemented cloud cost optimization strategies, reducing infrastructure costs through the utilization of reserved instances, rightsizing resources, and automating workload scaling based on demand.

Integration of Generative AI:

Integrated generative AI algorithms into the data analytics platform to enhance predictive analytics, fraud detection, and risk assessment capabilities, facilitating more effective identification of patterns and anomalies in financial transactions.

Outcome:

Enhanced Security and Compliance:

Implementation of cloud network security measures significantly bolstered the firm's security posture, ensuring compliance with regulatory requirements and safeguarding customer data from cyber threats.

Cost Savings and Operational Efficiency:

Efficient cost management strategies led to substantial savings, enabling the firm to allocate resources more effectively and invest in innovation and growth initiatives.

Improved Data Analytics and Risk Management:

Integration of generative AI improved data analytics capabilities, resulting in more accurate fraud detection, risk assessment, and predictive modelling, aiding in data-driven decision-making and mitigation of potential financial risks.

Competitive Advantage and Business Growth:

By leveraging cloud network security, efficient cost management, and generative AI, the financial services firm gained a competitive edge, enhancing customer trust, improving operational efficiency, and positioning itself for sustainable growth and expansion.

Chapter 7

Conclusion

In the journey of mastering any field, one often starts as a beginner, encountering challenges and uncertainties along the way. Just like me, who embarked on a path to understand the sophisticated dynamics of cloud security and cost management, business owners too can begin their expedition towards securing their business in the cloud.

In the beginning, it might seem disheartening, akin to navigating through uncharted territory. However, with each step taken and every lesson learned, I evolved from a beginner to an expert, unravelling the complexities of cloud security optimization and cost management. In my diverse experience of 20 years, my cloud journey commenced with Azure, where I delved into various services and comprehended their distinct purposes. At Accenture, I acquired expertise in comprehensive architecture design encompassing infrastructure, data, application, security, and integration. I gained insights into crucial factors to contemplate when crafting an architecture, including business requirements, scalability, availability, security, performance, cost, governance, data management, integration, monitoring, logging, disaster recovery, and backup. I crafted numerous integration designs tailored to diverse client needs. Concurrently, I spearheaded infrastructure and security architecture initiatives for internal projects while leading a dedicated team.

Transitioning to Wipro, I assumed leadership of the entire security team, contributing extensively to security architecture aligned with cost management strategies for transformation and migration endeavours. Subsequently, I led the operations team, providing guidance in the architecture and procurement of diverse services with a focus on cost optimization. Coming from a business-oriented family and being of the Baniya community, I've had the advantage of viewing everything through the lens of profit and loss analysis. My background in commerce has further enriched my understanding of cost management and profit optimization, adding valuable insights to my skill set. I had the opportunity to work in both delivery and competency concurrently, which enabled me to gain insights into solutions from multiple perspectives. Throughout my client engagements, I comprehended their pain points and delivered solutions tailored to their preferences and requirements. This included overseeing complete cloud security posture management across multiple cloud platforms like Azure, AWS, Oracle and Prisma cloud. I gained proficiency in delivering solutions tailored to both single-cloud and multi-cloud environments, prioritizing cost considerations. Additionally, I successfully implemented solutions based on Zero Trust architecture and defense-in-depth principles. I recognize the significance of Generative AI Security tools and their role across various layers of defensive mechanisms, aimed at minimizing threats and mitigating risks. Through diligence, dedication, and continuous learning, my expertise flourished, enabling me to offer valuable insights encapsulated in the book "Cost Savvy Secure Cloud"

Just as my journey exemplifies, business owner venture into cloud security and cost management holds immense potential to strengthen their business from both security breaches and unnecessary expenditures. By embracing the principles outlined in these invaluable resources, business owners can strategically choose the right cloud provider, strike a harmonious balance between network security and cost efficiency, and harness the transformative power of Generative AI.

As business owner delves into the chapters of wisdom laid out before them, remember that every exercise, case study, and real-world example serves as a beacon of insight, guiding them towards a future where their business thrives amidst the complexities of the digital landscape. Through governance, innovation, and a steadfast commitment to excellence, they have the opportunity to follow the success stories of enterprises that have redefined the paradigm of cloud security, cost management, and AI integration.

In conclusion, let my journey inspire business owners to embark on their own mission for mastery in cloud security and cost optimization. With dedication, knowledge, and the invaluable guidance of these profound resources, business owner possesses the keys to unlock a future where their business stands as a beacon of resilience, innovation, and prosperity in the ever-evolving realm of cloud technology.

Author Biography

Preity is a seasoned Multi-Cloud Business Security Strategist with over 20 years of extensive experience as Advisor, Consultant, Manager, and Architect, providing strategic direction for technology initiatives in alignment with business security compliance standards. She specializes in multi-cloud security, compliance management, risk assessment, and governance, guiding organizations towards secure cloud solutions. She is recognized for her visionary approach, robust analytical skills, and commitment to excellence.

With a background in Computer Applications and Commerce, Preity began her career as a Software Engineer, gaining experience in cloud-based software development, app modernisation, architecture designing, transformation and migration of data centre workloads, and multi-cloud security. Over the years, she has held various leadership roles in renowned organizations such as Wipro, Accenture, and HCL, where she led cloud transformative projects and provided strategic security guidance to clients across different industries.

Preity's expertise lies in leading cloud security transformation, migration, and operational projects, achieving significant cost savings while ensuring compliance with industry standards such as NIST, CIS Benchmark, GDPR, and ISO. She is known for her ability to establish strong collaborative relationships with clients and stakeholders, addressing their pain points and delivering innovative AI-enabled security solutions for multi-cloud environments.

Throughout her career, she has been recognized for her thought leadership in the cloud industry and her ability to nurture enduring customer relationships. She has received accolades for her contributions to project success, including Victory League and Accenture Excellence Awards. Passionate about continuous learning, Preity holds multiple certifications in cloud technologies and regularly attends training workshops to stay updated with the latest trends and innovations.

Preity holds a Master's degree in Computer Applications and Commerce from renowned universities. She is committed to leveraging her expertise and experience to drive innovation and excellence in the field of multi-cloud security and architecture. Currently, she is seeking opportunities to transition into a CxO role, where she can continue to make a significant impact in shaping the future of cloud security.

With a passion for excellence and a commitment to innovation, Preity continues to inspire and drive advancements in cloud security optimization with cost management and Generative AI.

Follow Preity on LinkedIn:
www.linkedin.com/in/preitygupta